Our books make helpful, evidence-based
mental health tools more accessible—made
by therapists, for everyone.

THERAPY NOTEBOOKS
www.therapynotebooks.com

THE FIELD GUIDE FOR DEPRESSION
Evidence-Based Tools to Motivate, Reframe, and Connect

Designed by therapists to help you discover the most
effective tools for managing depression.

. . . .
(THIS BOOK BELONGS TO)

. . . .
(IF FOUND, PLEASE RETURN TO)

LEARN MORE
www.therapynotebooks.com

THERAPY NOTEBOOKS
Published by Subject Matters

ISBN: 9781735084695
Printed in the United States of America

LEAD THERAPISTS
Diana Hu, PsyD
Hod Tamir, PhD

EDITED BY
Emory Strickland, PsyD
Meghan Nesmith
Emma Rosenberg

DESIGNED BY
Monumento.Co

BRANDING BY
High Tide

IF YOU ARE IN URGENT
NEED OF ASSISTANCE:
Dial 9-1-1

FOR MENTAL HEALTH
CRISIS SUPPORT:
Dial 9-8-8

SAMHSA National Helpline
1-800-622-HELP (4357)

Crisis Text Line
Text HOME to 741741

The book was designed
with your emotions in mind.

The entire book was designed to be helpful, no matter where or when you begin. We recommend making this book a part of your regular routine and working through the chapters in order, but there's no pressure.

So feel free to pause, skip around, or use as-needed.

We were guided by clinicians and mental health research.

We consulted experienced clinicians and interrogated the scientific evidence directly (with a focus on replicated, large, randomized controlled trials) in order to identify the tools most likely to help with depression. We have attempted to balance what is considered to be most trusted and effective with what will facilitate an intuitive and enjoyable experience.

Our hope: to help you discover the mental health tools that work for you.

Each section of this book introduces a new *evidence-based tool*, designed to improve your motivation, rewrite your internal dialogue, and foster connection in your relationships. Guidance from therapists and structured journal entries will empower you to put these tools into practice. You can learn more about each tool in the corresponding Appendices.

Overview of Tools

The tools in this book are each designed to help you with making specific changes and building related skills. They are arranged into three categories of change—below is an overview of what the tools are, how they can help you, and how we suggest practicing these tools.

GOAL	TOOL	PURPOSE
Improving Motivation	Acceptance and Commitment Therapy	Find meaning by connecting to your values
	Behavioral Activation	Pursue enjoyable activities to shift your mood
Improving Internal Dialogue	Cognitive Behavioral Therapy	Notice and challenge unhelpful thought patterns
	Growth Mindset	Believe in your potential for change
Improving Relationships	Dialectical Behavior Therapy	Practice setting boundaries to foster connection

* "Suggested use" is based on typical usage and practice, but ultimately what works best is what you find works well for you.

Letter From
a Therapist

We are bonded by certain universal emotions. At some point
we have all experienced feelings of fatigue, a lack of motivation,
a sense of worthlessness, or grief. But nowadays, whether due
to recent tragedies or wider cultural shifts, we are collectively
experiencing these depressing feelings more often and with
greater severity. Nearly 300 million people worldwide now
struggle with depression.[1] It has become the leading cause of
global disability, and some estimate nearly 20% of Americans
will deal with major depression at some point in their lives.[2]
Moreover, there has been a long standing stigma surrounding
mental health, particularly depression. External and internal
judgment about how we should feel—as if we're just lazy or
entitled—have prevented us from communicating about the
burden of pain imposed by feelings of depression.

Fortunately, there is reason for hope. The conversation
around mental health is changing and decades of mental health
research from psychology, psychiatry, and neuroscience have led
to the identification and development of tools that we know are
effective and can help. The American Psychological Association
lists nearly a dozen well-researched, evidence-based treatments
for depression (not including medications), and dozens of new
tools are currently being developed and studied.

But many people still lack access to therapy and trusted,
evidence-based tools. So as clinicians, we're excited to make
these tools more accessible. And ultimately we hope to get these
tools into more hands, and they can help more people feel better.
That is our goal.

This book is unique in that we offer a primer to some
of the most effective tools for depression—with the idea that
you can discover the tools that work best for you, rather than
us attempting to dictate what is best. We could not cover every
effective treatment in this edition, so we highlighted five of the
most well researched and widely trusted tools, and included
additional descriptions in the appendix. Also, we've intended
this book to be flexible: it can be used alongside other treatments
such as therapy or medication, or it can be used on its own.

Before jumping in, we hope you take a moment to recognize that simply beginning is a step forward. We want to honor

your desire to change, and the effort required to get to this page. Of course, this is not a magic wand—it will not miraculously make your worries disappear—but it will help you reflect, gain insight, and learn. We hope this process will remind you that you are capable of positive change. Every page you complete in this journal is an act of strength and courage. We're glad you're here.

Sincerely,

Diana Hu, PsyD & Hod Tamir, PhD
Lead Clinicians

Scan the QR code to
meet our clinicians

How This Book
Helps You

Experience five evidence-based tools highly effective for treating depression.

Get access to the most well-researched and expert-trusted tools to improve mood, relationships, and motivation—with hundreds of peer-reviewed studies to back them up.

2 Find what works for you.

Depression affects each of us in unique ways, and what works for one person may not be effective for you. We'll help you reflect on your experiences and experiment with a variety of tools to discover what works for you.

3 The right amount of structure and freedom to support your journaling.

Blank pages are daunting, and filling all that negative space can leave you at a loss for words. We've worked with experts to provide the right balance of structure and freedom to empower you to process your emotions and experiences effectively.

4 Discover the science behind the most effective tools.

Practicing the most well-researched tools for combatting depression is one thing—knowing why they work is another. In these pages, you'll be introduced to foundational research and principles behind depression and each evidence-based tool to empower you to experiment with what works.

5 Made by therapists with extensive experience treating depression.

Our empathetic, experienced clinicians hand-selected proven tools to help you learn how to clearly identify feelings, spot mental shortcuts, and find resources to expand your learning.

Contents

INTRODUCTION:
On Depression

Depression can feel demoralizing, sometimes even absurd. What was once an easy task, like leaving the house, requires all the will you can muster. Each step: getting out of bed, walking to the bathroom, taking a shower, putting on an outfit, and gathering our keys, feels herculean in scope. All the while, your mind becomes increasingly inhospitable. An inner voice tries to assert a cruel form of reason, "This shouldn't be so hard. What is wrong with you?" Of course, this only makes things worse.

You probably know this experience well, or know someone who does. One in ten of us will experience a major depression this year, and likely at least one in five in their lifetime.[3] Despite the remarkable prevalence of depression, more common than AIDS, cancer, and diabetes combined, the strange nature of the condition, paired with a societal reticence on the matter, can make us believe we are uniquely plagued.[4] "Nearly every depressed person seems convinced beyond all rhyme or reason" that they are "the special one who really is beyond hope," says Dr. David Burns.[5] No one is beyond hope, including you.

As unpleasant as the experience is, depression is not meaningless. It serves a function. In order to survive, our brains are constantly determining when we should exert energy. Sometimes, we come to the conclusion that our efforts are futile and, in response, our system shuts down.[6][7] By its own brutal logic, depression thinks it's doing us a favor. It protects us from further loss by muting our very ability to feel attached. Soon, what once brought us joy makes us feel... nothing.

Why some people go into this unhelpful protective mode, and others do not, is complicated. When it comes to the human experience, there's a lot we don't know. We know that losing a loved one, a job, or a relationship, or experiencing a personal crisis, injury, or financial stress can greatly increase your chance of experiencing depression.[8][9]

We know that depression is at least somewhat hereditary and have discovered specific genes that carry risk factors.[10] We know that depression, like all mental health disorders, impacts functions of brain circuits that regulate mood, pain, pleasure, and motivation.[11]

We also know that any answer—be it biological, psychological, philosophical, or otherwise—probably won't feel satisfying. At least, not enough to make the experience less uncomfortable. The brain craves clear answers when it is consumed by suffering. Please remember that no matter why your combination of life experience, biological makeup, and genetic predisposition has led you to this moment—there is a way forward.

The very mechanism that can make you believe life is futile is the same one that wants, desperately, to keep going. Your efforts, to read this book, to understand your depression, to learn about treatment options, to get up each morning, all make a difference. While we don't have perfect answers, and there is more research to be done, we do have evidence-based solutions that have helped real people. The odds are, there is something here that can work for you, too.

WHAT IS DEPRESSION?

What depression is depends on who you ask. Existential psychologist Rollo May once called depression "the inability to construct a future."[12] Martin Seligman, a positive psychologist, referred to depression as the "common cold of psychopathology." Freud believed depression, which he called melancholia, was a chronic form of grief, turning anger inward.[13] Some definitions of depression resonate on a human level, but are unscientific. Others take a more scientific approach, but can feel quite soulless. Biologist Robert Sapolsky attempted to bridge the gap: depression is "a biochemical disorder with a genetic component with early exposure experiences that make it so someone can't appreciate sunsets."[14]

The challenge is that the reason we feel depressed is under debate, and the disorder (sometimes called an illness or disease) is difficult to distinguish from its impact. Diagnoses are, after all, how the medical establishment attempts to categorize the complexities of the human experience. According to the American Psychiatric Association, "Depression (major depressive disorder) is a common and serious medical illness that negatively affects how you feel, the way you think and how you act."[3] The most recent Diagnostic and Statistical Manual of Mental Disorders (DSM) outlines a list of criteria to make a diagnosis of depression: "An individual must be experiencing five or more symptoms during the same two week period, and at least one of the symptoms should be either (1) depressed mood or (2) loss of interest or pleasure." Why five symptoms, and not four, two weeks, and not three, can feel quite arbitrary. Depression is hard to capture, but undeniable in its consequences.

In *Noonday Demon: An Atlas of Depression*, one of the most comprehensive accounts of depression written for the average reader, Andrew Solomon concludes that depression is more of a "symptom with symptoms" than a disease.[15] He compares the category of "depression" to "cough."

What is cough? We have decided to define cough as a symptom of various illnesses rather than as an illness of its own, though we can also look at what might be called the consequent symptoms of cough itself: sore throat, poor sleep, difficulty with speech, irritating tickly feelings, troubled breathing, and so on. Depression is not a rational disease category; like cough, it is a symptom with symptoms...

Recently, scientists at the National Institute of Mental Health (NIMH) adopted a new approach to diagnosis, called the Research Domain Criteria (RDoC).[16] The NIMH believes DSM categories are too expansive, which makes them more difficult to diagnose and treat. Instead of large categories like depression, which may be a "symptom with symptoms," RDoC breaks mental illnesses down into distinct biological and behavioral components. The RDoC components associated with depression include "anxious arousal," "attentional bias to threat," and "avoidance." One major premise of the RDoC is that all of these dysfunctions can, or will one day, be traced back to the brain or genetics, which will allow for even more targeted and effective treatments.

As with all things connected to the brain, with its 100 billion neurons and 10 trillion connections, and all trials of the human spirit, depression is nuanced. The diagnosis (or condition, illness, disease, and symptom with symptoms) is an umbrella term that captures innumerable individual experiences of people at their darkest hours. The good news is that you are not alone. We have more access to research than ever before to understand how depression works and what you can do to feel better.

WHY DO I HAVE IT?

Depression is complex, but we've made remarkable strides in understanding its etiology. In one of the largest genetic studies ever to be conducted, a gene variant related to serotonin was correlated with major depression.[17][18] A similarly large follow-up study in New Zealand showed that if you had the variant but experienced a relatively healthy childhood, you were at no greater risk than the average person for experiencing depression; however, if you experienced trauma or extreme stress, you were up to 30 times more likely to have depression.[19] The gene itself does not cause depression, but some complex interaction between the gene and environment greatly increases one's risk.

The gene studies are illustrative of two points. First, that depression may have no single cause, but like many other mental health disorders, it is provoked by a combination of triggers, vulnerabilities, and a lack of buffers, most outside our control. And second, that this combination of causes spans across biological, environmental, and social factors. A gene can introduce a vulnerability, but trauma may be a trigger. Sometimes stress from childhood trauma creates vulnerability, and brain development or later trauma may be the trigger. Stable social relationships are a well-established buffer for depression.[20] In fact, one other follow-up study of the same gene found those with more stable social relationships were much less likely to experience depression.[21]

Stressful life events, such as various types of loss and personal crises, have been shown to have a causal effect on depression.[8][9] Hormone balance likely plays a role: women are most at risk for depression during menstruation and after birth. [22] Low thyroid hormone levels can cause depression.[23] Lack of sleep can decrease activity of mood-regulating brain circuits and increases risk of depression.[24] Good sleep can be a buffer. Low socioeconomic status is one of the most predictive factors for depression.[25] Most researchers believe the depression from low socioeconomic status is a result of a combination of stressful life factors, a lack of access to adequate resources for assistance, and the known biological stress induced by having a lower status than peers.

The uncontrollable factors that are linked with depression can make it seem like the cards are stacked against us. But neither our genetic inheritance, childhood experiences, nor environmental forces seal our fate. As Helen Keller said, "Although the world is full of suffering, it is also full of the overcoming of it." Recovery begins with understanding what is within our control.

WHAT CAN I DO?

Depression does not play fair: the more depressed you are, the less equipped you feel to do the things that will help you get better. Your depressed brain might convince you it's best to wait it out until you feel like you have more will to take action. But healing from depression doesn't happen by chance. The process starts from within the belly of the beast, by accepting where we are and taking small and deliberate steps to change.

Today, you have more access to research-backed interventions than ever before. Modern science is not perfect, but within the last century advances in the field have led us from resorting to unproven conjectures and full lobotomies to at least a dozen evidence-based treatments and medications recognized by the American Psychiatric Association and other global health organizations. "Evidence-based" means rigorous studies were conducted to show, beyond chance alone, that these treatments can significantly reduce depression. When researchers deem a treatment is effective, they have studied the results of far more patients than a single clinician could treat alone. The sample sizes are large and randomized, so the researchers and participants did not choose which intervention they participated in. In short, countless people experiencing depression found actual relief from these methods, and you can, too.

Despite the volume of evidence available, treating your depression involves creativity and openness: to try various treatments, behaviors, and lifestyle changes and see what works. This experimental approach can be exasperating when you are desperate to feel better, but different people respond to different treatments. You just have to find the thing that works for you. You may even have a different response to the same tool depending on where you are in your journey; for example, you may find mindfulness to be too difficult at first, but later, it may become an essential component of your self-care routine. The path to recovery is often by way of a combination of modalities, persistence, and an underlying trust in the process.

Many people have found relief from antidepressants. Antidepressant medications have generally been found to be effective, though the exact mechanisms for how they work are still relatively unknown. Recent studies have shown combining these medications with evidence-based therapy yields even better results.[26] However, there are serious disagreements around pharmaceutical interventions because of their persistent side effects, withdrawal symptoms, and possible placebo effect. Some remain skeptical of the pharmaceutical industry's profit-driven incentives and institutional corruption. Newer, more targeted treatments are being developed every day, as well as physical interventions such as brain stimulation and transcranial magnetic stimulation. In recent years, there has also been a resurgence of psychedelic therapy, a transformative treatment that is gaining traction in the mental health community.

While there are numerous promising treatment options, not all of them can be accessed immediately, at your own pace, and from the comfort of your home. Our goal is to identify some of the most well-researched and evidence-based tools for depression that you can start practicing in this notebook. Through reading about the different tools and completing the journal entries, you are bound to find something that speaks to you. Each step you take to build your skills will start to create larger ripple effects in your life.

THERE IS HOPE

Depression is a treatable condition. We have numerous evidence-based tools that can help. It would be an understatement to say that recovering from depression is hard. The process is more trying than any job that could fit on someone's resume—but it is very much possible. The fact that you are reading this book is proof that you have hope for your recovery, or at the least, you are open to the possibility that you might feel hope in the future. Healing is not only within your reach, but completely worth the effort. What you will gain is more than just a reduction in symptoms, or the capacity to enjoy sunsets. Experiencing the very depths of human pain, and rising up from the ashes, will become the very thing that gives you a greater understanding of your own resilience, and a deeper appreciation for the full range of life's experiences.

Note From
a Therapist

Before getting started with the highlighted tools in the book, we wanted to draw your attention to some foundational aspects of mental health that we could not fully address.

FUNDAMENTALS OF SELF-CARE

There are fundamental aspects of mental health that nearly every clinician would emphasize as key buffers for depression and critical to your overall health: these include nutrition, exercise, sleep, physical health, and social connections.

We often take these fundamentals for granted and they also tend to get ignored the more depressed we feel. Paying attention to and setting up this foundation will help you learn and practice the upcoming tools more effectively. So we recommend looking through these fundamentals in Appendix B.

THERAPY AND OTHER TOOLS

This book is in no way a replacement for therapy or the work that can be accomplished with a licensed professional. If that type of treatment is accessible and interesting to you, we recommend reaching out to a clinician. Due to the limited nature of books, we focus on empowering you with knowledge and skills that clinicians and researchers trust.

TOOL I:
Acceptance and
Commitment Therapy

PRACTICE:
Values and Committed Action

Note From a Therapist

Acceptance and Commitment Therapy (ACT) helps you detach from unhelpful thoughts and focus on building the life you want. While it consists of six skills, we'll focus on two specific aspects that are especially helpful for cultivating a sense of purpose and internal motivation: Values and Committed Action. In the following exercises, you will (1) define your values more clearly and (2) commit to actions that will help you live your values.

VALUES

Values are guiding principles that help determine your actions. They are often traits that you want to embody or live by, such as "empathy," "openness," "comfort," or "adventure." Values are different from goals because while a goal can be met or checked off, living your values is a consistent practice that guides behavior on an ongoing basis. For instance, if you have the value of "justice," then your actions will continually be guided by choices that help you seek and promote justice in your life.

COMMITTED ACTION

Once you have identified your values, you'll name small, concrete, attainable steps on how you can embody them. It's okay if you haven't been living according to your values, you can commit now to making a change.

You can learn more about ACT by going to Appendix D.

How to Approach This Section

How Often: Complete in one or two sittings, 30-45 minutes.

When: While feeling calm and rested.

Tips: Values: Remember, these need to be your values. There's no "right" or "wrong" value, and these don't need to match what you think others want from you. Feel free to get really honest with yourself about what you find most important.

              Committed Action: It's important to be specific and to keep in mind that small actions are more attainable, less daunting, and are more likely to build towards an ongoing practice.

PART I:
Exploring Your Values

Circle the values* that feel the most important to you (we recommend choosing approximately 10). In the next section, we'll narrow things down further.

1.   Accepting: open to, allowing of, or at peace with myself, others, life, my feelings, etc.

2.   Adventurous: willing to create or pursue novel, risky, or exciting experiences

3.   Assertive: calmly, fairly and respectfully standing up for my rights and asking for what I want

4.   Authentic: being genuine, real, and true to myself

5.   Caring/self-caring: actively taking care of myself, others, the environment, etc.

6.   Compassionate/self-compassionate: responding kindly to myself or others in pain

7.   Cooperative: willing to assist and work with others

8.   Courageous: being brave or bold; persisting in the face of fear, threat, or risk

9.   Creative: being imaginative, inventive, or innovative

10.   Curious: being open-minded and interested; willing to explore and discover

11.   Encouraging: supporting, inspiring, and rewarding behavior I approve of

12.   Expressive: conveying my thoughts and feelings through what I say and do

13.   Focused: focused on and engaged in what I am doing

14. Fair/just: acting with fairness and justice—toward myself and others

15. Flexible: willing and able to adjust and adapt to changing circumstances

16. Friendly: warm, open, caring, and agreeable toward others

17. Forgiving: letting go of resentments and grudges toward myself or others

18. Grateful: being appreciative for what I have received

19. Helpful: giving, helping, contributing, assisting, or sharing

20. Honest: being honest, truthful, and sincere—with myself and others

21. Independent: choosing for myself how I live and what I do

22. Industrious: being diligent, hardworking, dedicated

23. Kind: being considerate, helpful, or caring—to myself or others

24. Loving: showing love, affection, or great care—to myself or others

25. Mindful or present: fully present and engaging in whatever I'm doing

26. Open: revealing myself, letting people know my thoughts and feelings

27. Orderly: being neat and organized

28. Persistent/committed: willing to continue, despite problems or difficulties

29. Playful: being humorous, fun-loving, light-hearted

30. Protective: looking after the safety and security of myself or others

31. Respectful/self-respectful: treating myself or others with care and consideration

32. Responsible: being trustworthy, reliable, and accountable for my actions

33. Skillful: doing things well, utilizing my knowledge, experience, and training

34. Supportive: being helpful, encouraging, and available—to myself or others

35.   Trustworthy: being loyal, honest, faithful, sincere, responsible, and reliable

36.   Trusting: willing to believe in the honesty, sincerity, reliability, or competence of another

Others

(Feel free to add values you may have that are not listed)

* This list of values and definitions are credited to R. Harris's ACT Made Simple[27]

PART II:
Top Values

Narrow down your top 3-4 most important values (they don't have to be in order). In the next section, you'll have a chance to reflect on why these values are important to you.

-
-
-
-

PART III:
Reflecting on Your Values

For each of your most important values, reflect on why
they're important to you, and start imagining what a more
value-driven life might look like. On the next page is an example
and some helpful tips.

What is the value?

Instructions: List one of your top values here to explore it further.

Example: Compassion.

2   Why is this value so important to you?

Instructions: Explore what makes this value so important to you or why it resonated so
deeply with you.

Example: I want for people to feel that they can come to me and that I will hear them out and
be understanding. I want to show that I believe people are doing their best. This is a trait I
see in others that strengthens their relationships and helps them feel more connected, and
I'd like to emulate that.

3   What does living a life aligned with this value look like to you?
        (Consider your relationships, work life, and other important areas of your life).

Instructions: Name what kinds of behaviors or attitudes might come with living a life with
this value. Consider how this might look across several important aspects of your life.

Example: I want to act with greater kindness and patience, with my family and myself.
Acting with compassion would mean that I am more present with my loved ones.

4   Reflect on your daily life: what are some ways you are already living by this value
        and what are some ways you could improve?

Instructions: Consider what concrete action(s) you could bring to your day-to-day life from
this value. Identify ways or situations in which you may already be aligned with this value,
and when you may have the opportunity to practice this value. Even one small step can be
meaningful.

Example: This value would mean putting down my phone when I'm talking to people, and
asking more follow-up questions about what they're saying. I'm already good at doing this
at work, and people notice that I am curious. I tend to be more short-fused with my parents,
and could take a few breaths when getting worked up with them in particular.

1   What is the value?

2   Why is this value so important to you?

3   What does living a life aligned with this value look like to you?
        (Consider your relationships, work life, and other important areas of your life).

4   Reflect on your daily life: what are some ways you are already living by this value
        and what are some ways you could improve?

1 What is the value?

2 Why is this value so important to you?

3 What does living a life aligned with this value look like to you?
(Consider your relationships, work life, and other important areas of your life).

4 Reflect on your daily life: what are some ways you are already living by this value
and what are some ways you could improve?

1   What is the value?

2   Why is this value so important to you?

3   What does living a life aligned with this value look like to you?
         (Consider your relationships, work life, and other important areas of your life).

4   Reflect on your daily life: what are some ways you are already living by this value
         and what are some ways you could improve?

1   What is the value?

2   Why is this value so important to you?

3   What does living a life aligned with this value look like to you?
        (Consider your relationships, work life, and other important areas of your life).

4   Reflect on your daily life: what are some ways you are already living by this value
        and what are some ways you could improve?

PART IV:
Committed Action

Next, we'll pick two values from the previous section that you'd most like to develop and start planning specific actions you can take to live a life closer to your values.

1   What is the value?

Instructions: Write one of your top values from the previous exercise.

Example: Self-Respectful.

2   What's one act you can commit to?

Instructions: Name an action or behavior you can do in the next day or two.
Be as specific as possible in identifying what you will do, when, and how.

Example: I will take better care of my nutrition. I will eat when I start to feel hungry. If it's
not close to my lunch break, I can have a snack that's easy to eat while I'm working, or a
smoothie/drink. If it's while I'm in a meeting, I can ask at the beginning if it's okay, or have an
energy bar or small snack available.

3   What challenges do you anticipate? What can you do to prepare?

Instructions: List any physical obstacles, difficult feelings, or thoughts you can anticipate.
Consider what can be done to overcome those challenges. If not much can be done, think of
reminders that will help you accept the difficulty in the moment.

Example: It might feel awkward to ask if I can eat, so I'll keep small snacks in my bag that
can be quickly consumed. But if I still feel hungry during a meeting and haven't eaten, I will
remind myself that this is a priority and that taking care of my health is also part of fostering
a supportive work environment, which is important to me and the team.

1   What is the value?

2   What's one act you can commit to?

3   What challenges do you anticipate? What can you do to prepare?

What is the value?

What's one act you can commit to?

What challenges do you anticipate? What can you do to prepare?

TOOL II:
Behavioral Activation

PRACTICE:
Activity Log

Note From a Therapist

Behavioral Activation is about doing small things to shift your mood. This can be difficult to engage with especially when you feel little energy or desire to do anything, but it is one of the most frequently used and trusted tools for depression. Research consistently shows that just doing something, no matter how small the action, can help you get unstuck, shift your mood, and feel better.

For these BA exercises, you will be planning activities and tracking how they made you feel. Tracking will help you generate even more momentum as you identify which are working well for you, and it will challenge the idea that nothing can change how you feel.

We've provided examples of activities to get you started. The activities you choose should be specific, concrete, and achievable for you—not just things that you ideally "should" do.

You may occasionally experience self-judgmental thoughts, such as "It took me way too long to do this," or "I'm terrible for requiring so much effort." In this exercise, try to accept wherever you are and whatever feels difficult. It doesn't matter how much effort something takes; it only matters what you notice and how you feel while doing it.

You can learn more about Behavioral Activation by going to Appendix E.

How to Approach This Section

How Often: Daily if possible, or a few times a week.

When: Any state of mind—this helps strengthen the belief that taking action doesn't have to depend on your mood.

Tips: As you list specific actions, it may help to remember the SMART acronym: specific, measurable, achievable, realistic, and timely. Instead of a broad task such as "I want to take better care of myself," try to be more specific, such as "I will go for a 10 minute walk after lunch." This increases the likelihood that you will accomplish the task. If in doubt, set the smallest action you can think of, with more time to complete it than you think you need.

You may find the values and committed action work from the previous section can help direct you towards certain activities that you'll find more internally motivating and significant.

Examples of Activities

Feel free to circle the ones that sound more accessible
to you, as a starting point for future journal entries.

Walk or jog for 10 minutes
Listen to a favorite album or playlist
Organize a cluttered area
Sit or lay in the sun
Watch a funny video or TV episode
Thanking someone for something
Look at photos of fun past trips
Read a magazine or news article
Pay for the drink of the person after you in a drive-thru coffee shop
Eat a snack or meal you enjoy
Repair or clean something in the house
Try on an interesting outfit
Cuddle a pet
Take care of your plants
Call a friend
Dance
Plan coffee or a meal with a friend
Clear out storage on phone/computer
Go on a bike ride
Make a meal
Sing along to a favorite song
Create a budget
Pick out old clothes/books/toys to donate
Buy flowers

Go to the beach or pool

Message an old friend

Listen to an audiobook chapter or podcast

Go for a drive

Tidy up a room

Take a bath

Try something new, like a recipe, dance move, or yoga pose

Work on a jigsaw puzzle

Make a donation to a charity you like

Light a scented candle

Write a letter or card to someone

Specific values-based actions from ACT section

Before: Plan Something

1   Date:

Instructions: Name the day you'd like to complete the activity.

Example: Saturday

2   What activity will you do?

Instructions: Be as specific as possible.

Example: Buy groceries for the week (bulk breakfast items, 5 lunches and dinners).

3   When will you do it?   (Fill in time or benchmark activity)

Instructions: Name the most realistic time for you to complete this.

Example: Make a list in the morning, go to the store right after.

4   How long will it take?

Instructions: Set an attainable length of time for you to be doing this activity.

Example: As long as it takes, or a few hours.

5   Where will you do it?

Instructions: Identify the location for this that best meets your needs.

Example: Safeway is closest to me and probably has everything I need.

6   List key barriers that you might encounter.

Instructions: List what might get in your way of completing this.

Example: Might be hard to think about what meals to put together. Might wake up not feeling like doing it all.

7   What might you think or do to overcome these barriers?

Instructions: Given those barriers, identify possible solutions, workarounds, or reminders for yourself.

Example: I just need a protein, a veg, and a starch for each dinner, and lunches can be leftovers, or easy

meals I buy. I can buy pre-prepped or frozen foods to put together, and maybe also frozen meals. I might

not feel like it, but if I go, I won't need to go again for the week.

After: Track How It Went

Instructions: Rate your activity based on your mood, sense of achievement, and feeling of joy. Even noticing slight improvements can be helpful.

Mood: How much did it improve your mood?			(Circle one)
Not at all	(A little)	Somewhat	A lot

Achievement: How much did it improve your sense of achievement?			(Circle one)
(Not at all)	A little	Somewhat	A lot

Joy: How much did it improve your sense of joy?			(Circle one)
Not at all	A little	(Somewhat)	A lot

Any additional thoughts on how it went or what it was like?

Instructions: This is a space for you to process. What did you notice through planning and completing the activity? What did you expect before doing it? How was that different from how it went?

Example: I definitely thought that this was both stupidly easy and really overwhelming to do. That's why I've been feeling really guilty about not doing it. I thought I would hate dragging myself to the store and wandering through the aisles, but it wasn't so bad. I got anxious when I had to choose certain items, but overall I'm glad that I went and now I feel more prepared for the week.

Before: Plan Something

1   Date:

2   What activity will you do?

3   When will you do it?   (Fill in time or benchmark activity)

4   How long will it take?

5   Where will you do it?

6   List key barriers that you might encounter.

7   What might you think or do to overcome these barriers?

After: Track How It Went

Mood: How much did it improve your mood?			(Circle one)
Not at all	A little	Somewhat	A lot

Achievement: How much did it improve your sense of achievement?			(Circle one)
Not at all	A little	Somewhat	A lot

Joy: How much did it improve your sense of joy?			(Circle one)
Not at all	A little	Somewhat	A lot

Any additional thoughts on how it went or what it was like?

Before: Plan Something

1   Date:

2   What activity will you do?

3   When will you do it?   (Fill in time or benchmark activity)

4   How long will it take?

5   Where will you do it?

6   List key barriers that you might encounter.

7   What might you think or do to overcome these barriers?

After: Track How It Went

1   Mood: How much did it improve your mood?   (Circle one)

Not at all   A little   Somewhat   A lot

2   Achievement: How much did it improve your sense of achievement?   (Circle one)

Not at all   A little   Somewhat   A lot

3   Joy: How much did it improve your sense of joy?   (Circle one)

Not at all   A little   Somewhat   A lot

4   Any additional thoughts on how it went or what it was like?

Before: Plan Something

1   Date:

2   What activity will you do?

3   When will you do it?   (Fill in time or benchmark activity)

4   How long will it take?

5   Where will you do it?

6   List key barriers that you might encounter.

7   What might you think or do to overcome these barriers?

After: Track How It Went

Mood: How much did it improve your mood?			(Circle one)
Not at all	A little	Somewhat	A lot

Achievement: How much did it improve your sense of achievement?			(Circle one)
Not at all	A little	Somewhat	A lot

Joy: How much did it improve your sense of joy?			(Circle one)
Not at all	A little	Somewhat	A lot

Any additional thoughts on how it went or what it was like?

Before: Plan Something

1   Date: _____

2   What activity will you do? _____

3   When will you do it? _____ (Fill in time or benchmark activity)

4   How long will it take? _____

5   Where will you do it? _____

6   List key barriers that you might encounter. _____

7   What might you think or do to overcome these barriers? ____

After: Track How It Went

Mood: How much did it improve your mood?			(Circle one)
Not at all	A little	Somewhat	A lot

Achievement: How much did it improve your sense of achievement?			(Circle one)
Not at all	A little	Somewhat	A lot

Joy: How much did it improve your sense of joy?			(Circle one)
Not at all	A little	Somewhat	A lot

Any additional thoughts on how it went or what it was like?

Before: Plan Something

1   Date:

2   What activity will you do?

3   When will you do it?   (Fill in time or benchmark activit

4   How long will it take?

5   Where will you do it?

6   List key barriers that you might encounter.

7   What might you think or do to overcome these barriers?

After: Track How It Went

Mood: How much did it improve your mood?			(Circle one)
Not at all	A little	Somewhat	A lot

Achievement: How much did it improve your sense of achievement?			(Circle one)
Not at all	A little	Somewhat	A lot

Joy: How much did it improve your sense of joy?			(Circle one)
Not at all	A little	Somewhat	A lot

Any additional thoughts on how it went or what it was like?

Before: Plan Something

1   Date:

2   What activity will you do?

3   When will you do it?   (Fill in time or benchmark activit

4   How long will it take?

5   Where will you do it?

6   List key barriers that you might encounter.

7   What might you think or do to overcome these barriers?

After: Track How It Went

Mood: How much did it improve your mood?			(Circle one)
Not at all	A little	Somewhat	A lot

Achievement: How much did it improve your sense of achievement?			(Circle one)
Not at all	A little	Somewhat	A lot

Joy: How much did it improve your sense of joy?			(Circle one)
Not at all	A little	Somewhat	A lot

Any additional thoughts on how it went or what it was like?

Before: Plan Something

1   Date:

2   What activity will you do?

3   When will you do it?   (Fill in time or benchmark activity)

4   How long will it take?

5   Where will you do it?

6   List key barriers that you might encounter.

7   What might you think or do to overcome these barriers?

After: Track How It Went

Mood: How much did it improve your mood?			(Circle one)
Not at all	A little	Somewhat	A lot

Achievement: How much did it improve your sense of achievement?			(Circle one)
Not at all	A little	Somewhat	A lot

Joy: How much did it improve your sense of joy?			(Circle one)
Not at all	A little	Somewhat	A lot

Any additional thoughts on how it went or what it was like?

Before: Plan Something

1   Date:

2   What activity will you do?

3   When will you do it?   (Fill in time or benchmark activity

4   How long will it take?

5   Where will you do it?

6   List key barriers that you might encounter.

7   What might you think or do to overcome these barriers?

After: Track How It Went

Mood: How much did it improve your mood?			(Circle one)
Not at all	A little	Somewhat	A lot

Achievement: How much did it improve your sense of achievement?			(Circle one)
Not at all	A little	Somewhat	A lot

Joy: How much did it improve your sense of joy?			(Circle one)
Not at all	A little	Somewhat	A lot

Any additional thoughts on how it went or what it was like?

Before: Plan Something

1   Date: _____

2   What activity will you do? _____

3   When will you do it? _____ (Fill in time or benchmark activity|

4   How long will it take? _____

5   Where will you do it? _____

6   List key barriers that you might encounter. _____

7   What might you think or do to overcome these barriers? ___

After: Track How It Went

Mood: How much did it improve your mood?			(Circle one)
Not at all	A little	Somewhat	A lot

Achievement: How much did it improve your sense of achievement?			(Circle one)
Not at all	A little	Somewhat	A lot

Joy: How much did it improve your sense of joy?			(Circle one)
Not at all	A little	Somewhat	A lot

Any additional thoughts on how it went or what it was like?

Before: Plan Something

1   Date:

2   What activity will you do?

3   When will you do it?   (Fill in time or benchmark activity)

4   How long will it take?

5   Where will you do it?

6   List key barriers that you might encounter.

7   What might you think or do to overcome these barriers?

After: Track How It Went

Mood: How much did it improve your mood?			(Circle one)
Not at all	A little	Somewhat	A lot

Achievement: How much did it improve your sense of achievement?			(Circle one)
Not at all	A little	Somewhat	A lot

Joy: How much did it improve your sense of joy?			(Circle one)
Not at all	A little	Somewhat	A lot

Any additional thoughts on how it went or what it was like?

Before: Plan Something

1   Date:

2   What activity will you do?

3   When will you do it?   (Fill in time or benchmark activity

4   How long will it take?

5   Where will you do it?

6   List key barriers that you might encounter.

7   What might you think or do to overcome these barriers?

After: Track How It Went

Mood: How much did it improve your mood?			(Circle one)
Not at all	A little	Somewhat	A lot

Achievement: How much did it improve your sense of achievement?			(Circle one)
Not at all	A little	Somewhat	A lot

Joy: How much did it improve your sense of joy?			(Circle one)
Not at all	A little	Somewhat	A lot

Any additional thoughts on how it went or what it was like?

Before: Plan Something

1   Date:

2   What activity will you do?

3   When will you do it?   (Fill in time or benchmark activity)

4   How long will it take?

5   Where will you do it?

6   List key barriers that you might encounter.

7   What might you think or do to overcome these barriers?

After: Track How It Went

Mood: How much did it improve your mood?			(Circle one)
Not at all	A little	Somewhat	A lot

Achievement: How much did it improve your sense of achievement?			(Circle one)
Not at all	A little	Somewhat	A lot

Joy: How much did it improve your sense of joy?			(Circle one)
Not at all	A little	Somewhat	A lot

Any additional thoughts on how it went or what it was like?

Before: Plan Something

1   Date:

2   What activity will you do?

3   When will you do it?   (Fill in time or benchmark activit

4   How long will it take?

5   Where will you do it?

6   List key barriers that you might encounter.

7   What might you think or do to overcome these barriers?

After: Track How It Went

Mood: How much did it improve your mood?   (Circle one)

Not at all   A little   Somewhat   A lot

Achievement: How much did it improve your sense of achievement?   (Circle one)

Not at all   A little   Somewhat   A lot

Joy: How much did it improve your sense of joy?   (Circle one)

Not at all   A little   Somewhat   A lot

Any additional thoughts on how it went or what it was like?

Before: Plan Something

1   Date:

2   What activity will you do?

3   When will you do it?   (Fill in time or benchmark activit

4   How long will it take?

5   Where will you do it?

6   List key barriers that you might encounter.

7   What might you think or do to overcome these barriers?

After: Track How It Went

Mood: How much did it improve your mood?			(Circle one)
Not at all	A little	Somewhat	A lot

Achievement: How much did it improve your sense of achievement?			(Circle one)
Not at all	A little	Somewhat	A lot

Joy: How much did it improve your sense of joy?			(Circle one)
Not at all	A little	Somewhat	A lot

Any additional thoughts on how it went or what it was like?

Before: Plan Something

1   Date:

2   What activity will you do?

3   When will you do it?   (Fill in time or benchmark activity)

4   How long will it take?

5   Where will you do it?

6   List key barriers that you might encounter.

7   What might you think or do to overcome these barriers?

After: Track How It Went

Mood: How much did it improve your mood?			(Circle one)
Not at all	A little	Somewhat	A lot

Achievement: How much did it improve your sense of achievement?			(Circle one)
Not at all	A little	Somewhat	A lot

Joy: How much did it improve your sense of joy?			(Circle one)
Not at all	A little	Somewhat	A lot

Any additional thoughts on how it went or what it was like?

Before: Plan Something

1   Date:

2   What activity will you do?

3   When will you do it?   (Fill in time or benchmark activity)

4   How long will it take?

5   Where will you do it?

6   List key barriers that you might encounter.

7   What might you think or do to overcome these barriers?

After: Track How It Went

Mood: How much did it improve your mood?			(Circle one)
Not at all	A little	Somewhat	A lot

Achievement: How much did it improve your sense of achievement?			(Circle one)
Not at all	A little	Somewhat	A lot

Joy: How much did it improve your sense of joy?			(Circle one)
Not at all	A little	Somewhat	A lot

Any additional thoughts on how it went or what it was like?

Before: Plan Something

1   Date:

2   What activity will you do?

3   When will you do it?   (Fill in time or benchmark activity)

4   How long will it take?

5   Where will you do it?

6   List key barriers that you might encounter.

7   What might you think or do to overcome these barriers?

After: Track How It Went

Mood: How much did it improve your mood?			(Circle one)
Not at all	A little	Somewhat	A lot

Achievement: How much did it improve your sense of achievement?			(Circle one)
Not at all	A little	Somewhat	A lot

Joy: How much did it improve your sense of joy?			(Circle one)
Not at all	A little	Somewhat	A lot

Any additional thoughts on how it went or what it was like?

Before: Plan Something

1   Date:

2   What activity will you do?

3   When will you do it?   (Fill in time or benchmark activity)

4   How long will it take?

5   Where will you do it?

6   List key barriers that you might encounter.

7   What might you think or do to overcome these barriers?

After: Track How It Went

Mood: How much did it improve your mood?			(Circle one)
Not at all	A little	Somewhat	A lot

Achievement: How much did it improve your sense of achievement?			(Circle one)
Not at all	A little	Somewhat	A lot

Joy: How much did it improve your sense of joy?			(Circle one)
Not at all	A little	Somewhat	A lot

Any additional thoughts on how it went or what it was like?

Before: Plan Something

1   Date:

2   What activity will you do?

3   When will you do it?   (Fill in time or benchmark activity)

4   How long will it take?

5   Where will you do it?

6   List key barriers that you might encounter.

7   What might you think or do to overcome these barriers?

After: Track How It Went

Mood: How much did it improve your mood?   (Circle one)

Not at all   A little   Somewhat   A lot

Achievement: How much did it improve your sense of achievement?   (Circle one)

Not at all   A little   Somewhat   A lot

Joy: How much did it improve your sense of joy?   (Circle one)

Not at all   A little   Somewhat   A lot

Any additional thoughts on how it went or what it was like?

Before: Plan Something

1   Date:

2   What activity will you do?

3   When will you do it?   (Fill in time or benchmark activity)

4   How long will it take?

5   Where will you do it?

6   List key barriers that you might encounter.

7   What might you think or do to overcome these barriers?

After: Track How It Went

Mood: How much did it improve your mood?   (Circle one)

Not at all   A little   Somewhat   A lot

Achievement: How much did it improve your sense of achievement?   (Circle one)

Not at all   A little   Somewhat   A lot

Joy: How much did it improve your sense of joy?   (Circle one)

Not at all   A little   Somewhat   A lot

Any additional thoughts on how it went or what it was like?

TOOL III:
Cognitive Behavioral Therapy

PRACTICE:
Thought Log

Note From
a Therapist

CBT helps you look at your thoughts more objectively and create space between a situation and the automatic thoughts and feelings that arise from it. By becoming aware of your thoughts and feelings you can begin to challenge them, notice inaccurate patterns, and change them for the better. The next exercise is one particularly popular tool within CBT called the "Thought Log."

The Thought Log helps you understand which automatic thought patterns your mind most often gravitates to, and helps you practice looking at the situation with greater clarity and nuance. You'll identify a difficult moment and list some of your corresponding thoughts. Then you'll label which automatic thought pattern was used (CBT refers to these as Cognitive Distortions). Finally, you'll practice reframing the thought to be more helpful and truthful. A memorable mnemonic: "Check it, Challenge it, Change it."

A list of various cognitive distortions, including examples, is provided in Appendix A of this book. Please take a moment to look over them. You can also learn more about CBT by going to Appendix F.

How to Approach
This Section

How Often: Weekly, or more often as desired.

When: As needed during difficult moments.

                  People tend to use the thought log journal
                  entry as they encounter distressing moments
                  or low moods throughout the day. For some
                  that may be multiple times a day, and for
                  some only a few times a week.

Tips: It may be helpful to bookmark Appendix A for
                  reference as you go through these exercises.

                  See if you can recognize when you are having
                  secondary reactions (thoughts or feelings in
                  response to your immediate reaction), and
                  target your journal entry to just one reaction.

                  If you notice that some feelings (i.e. sad,
                  frustrated, or anxious) come up regularly for
                  you, see if there are nuances to the feelings
                  that you can identify (i.e. disappointment,
                  anger, fear, etc).

1   What happened?   (Describe the situatior

Instructions: Try to focus on the facts (who, what, when, where). Be brief and specific. The smaller the moment in time you can pinpoint, the better you'll understand the emotions and reactions that followed

Example: At dinner, Jesse's mom made a joke about my job. Something about being an hourly worker. His whole family was there and everyone laughed.

2   What is going through your mind?   (Describe the situatior

Instructions: Put yourself back in that moment and note the thoughts that were in your head. Identi-fying your thoughts is a foundational aspect of CBT. Instead of dismissing your thoughts (e.g. "it really wasn't that big of a deal"), allow them to flow honestly.

Example: I immediately thought, why did she say that? Does everyone think I have a terrible job? I wondered if Jesse's entire family thinks I'm mooching off my partner or that he deserves better. Honestly, I thought maybe I really can't get a better job and Jesse might leave me eventually.

3   What emotions are you feeling?   (Note the intensity

Instructions: Name the various emotions you felt in that moment. Rate their intensity on a scale from 1 (barely feeling the emotion) to 10 (most intensely you've ever felt this way). Use the Feelings Wheel in Appendix A for help.

Example:

Ashamed   1 2 3 4 5 6 (7) 8 9 1C

Hurt   1 2 3 4 5 6 7 (8) 9 1C

4   What thought patterns do you recognize?   (Circle any or write your own

Instructions: Naming our thought patterns helps us see how our self-talk may be skewed and begin reducing some of the emotional intensity. Consult the Cognitive Distortions section in Appendix A to see definitions of common patterns.

Example:

All or nothing	(Fortune telling)	Minimizing the positive
Blaming others	Labeling	Overgeneralization
(Catastrophizing)	Magnifying the negative	(Self-blaming)
Emotional reasoning	(Mind reading)	Should statements

How can you think about the situation differently?   (Challenge your thoughts)

Instructions: Taking a step back from automatically believing our thoughts is the hard work of CBT.
Try to take a more objective, helpful, and self-compassionate look at your thoughts and patterns.

Example: Jesse's mom's comment hurt, but she's never made a comment about my job before and
it was likely just a joke. I really enjoy my job. Also, Jesse's family has consistently welcomed me into
their home and been friendly. It doesn't matter if they care how much I make. I make Jesse happy
and we have a healthy relationship.

Make note of any additional reflections you have.

Instructions: This is your space. We encourage you to use it however you wish.

A few suggestions:

- Draw, sketch, scribble, or free write
- Continue your answers from the previous section
- List one small concrete action you can take now or later that might make you feel better

1   What happened?   (Describe the situation

2   What is going through your mind?   (Describe the situation

3   What emotions are you feeling?   (Note the intensity)

1 2 3 4 5 6 7 8 9 10

1 2 3 4 5 6 7 8 9 10

1 2 3 4 5 6 7 8 9 10

4   What thought patterns do you recognize?   (Circle any or write your own)

All or nothing	Fortune telling	Minimizing the positive
Blaming others	Labeling	Overgeneralization
Catastrophizing	Magnifying the negative	Self-blaming
Emotional reasoning	Mind reading	Should statements

How can you think about the situation differently?   (Challenge your thoughts)

Make note of any additional reflections you have.

1   What happened?   (Describe the situation

. . . .

. . . .

. . . .

. . . .

. . . .

2   What is going through your mind?   (Describe the situation

. . . .

. . . .

. . . .

. . . .

. . . .

3   What emotions are you feeling?   (Note the intensity

                                          1 2 3 4 5 6 7 8 9 1
. . . .
                                          1 2 3 4 5 6 7 8 9 1
. . . .
                                          1 2 3 4 5 6 7 8 9 1
. . . .

. . . .

. . . .

4   What thought patterns do you recognize?   (Circle any or write your own

All or nothing   Fortune telling   Minimizing the positive
Blaming others   Labeling   Overgeneralization
Catastrophizing   Magnifying the negative   Self-blaming
Emotional reasoning   Mind reading   Should statements

. . . .

. . . .

. . . .

. . . .

. . . .

How can you think about the situation differently?   (Challenge your thoughts)

Make note of any additional reflections you have.

1   What happened?   (Describe the situatio

. . . .

. . . .

. . . .

. . . .

. . . .

2   What is going through your mind?   (Describe the situatio

. . . .

. . . .

. . . .

. . . .

. . . .

3   What emotions are you feeling?   (Note the intensit

                                        1 2 3 4 5 6 7 8 9 1
. . . .   1 2 3 4 5 6 7 8 9 1
. . . .   1 2 3 4 5 6 7 8 9 1

. . . .

. . . .

4   What thought patterns do you recognize?   (Circle any or write your ow

       All or nothing   Fortune telling   Minimizing the positiv
       Blaming others   Labeling   Overgeneralization
       Catastrophizing   Magnifying the negative   Self-blaming
       Emotional reasoning   Mind reading   Should statements

. . . .

. . . .

. . . .

. . . .

. . . .

How can you think about the situation differently?   (Challenge your thoughts)

Make note of any additional reflections you have.

1   What happened?   (Describe the situation

2   What is going through your mind?   (Describe the situation

3   What emotions are you feeling?   (Note the intensity

1 2 3 4 5 6 7 8 9 10

1 2 3 4 5 6 7 8 9 10

1 2 3 4 5 6 7 8 9 10

4   What thought patterns do you recognize?   (Circle any or write your own

All or nothing	Fortune telling	Minimizing the positive
Blaming others	Labeling	Overgeneralization
Catastrophizing	Magnifying the negative	Self-blaming
Emotional reasoning	Mind reading	Should statements

How can you think about the situation differently?   (Challenge your thoughts)

Make note of any additional reflections you have.

1   What happened?   (Describe the situation

2   What is going through your mind?   (Describe the situation

3   What emotions are you feeling?   (Note the intensity

1 2 3 4 5 6 7 8 9 10

1 2 3 4 5 6 7 8 9 10

1 2 3 4 5 6 7 8 9 10

4   What thought patterns do you recognize?   (Circle any or write your own

All or nothing	Fortune telling	Minimizing the positive
Blaming others	Labeling	Overgeneralization
Catastrophizing	Magnifying the negative	Self-blaming
Emotional reasoning	Mind reading	Should statements

How can you think about the situation differently?   (Challenge your thoughts)

Make note of any additional reflections you have.

1   What happened?   (Describe the situatio

2   What is going through your mind?   (Describe the situatio

3   What emotions are you feeling?   (Note the intensi

1 2 3 4 5 6 7 8 9

1 2 3 4 5 6 7 8 9

1 2 3 4 5 6 7 8 9

4   What thought patterns do you recognize?   (Circle any or write your ow

All or nothing   Fortune telling   Minimizing the positiv
Blaming others   Labeling   Overgeneralization
Catastrophizing   Magnifying the negative   Self-blaming
Emotional reasoning   Mind reading   Should statements

How can you think about the situation differently?   (Challenge your thoughts)

Make note of any additional reflections you have.

1   What happened?   (Describe the situatio

. . . .

. . . .

. . . .

. . . .

. . . .

2   What is going through your mind?   (Describe the situatio

. . . .

. . . .

. . . .

. . . .

. . . .

3   What emotions are you feeling?   (Note the intensi

                                                1 2 3 4 5 6 7 8 9
. . . .
                                                1 2 3 4 5 6 7 8 9
. . . .
                                                1 2 3 4 5 6 7 8 9
. . . .

. . . .

. . . .

4   What thought patterns do you recognize?   (Circle any or write your ow

        All or nothing   Fortune telling   Minimizing the positi
        Blaming others   Labeling   Overgeneralization
        Catastrophizing   Magnifying the negative   Self-blaming
        Emotional reasoning   Mind reading   Should statements

. . . .

. . . .

. . . .

. . . .

. . . .

5   How can you think about the situation differently?   (Challenge your thoughts)

6   Make note of any additional reflections you have.

1   What happened?   (Describe the situation

2   What is going through your mind?   (Describe the situation

3   What emotions are you feeling?   (Note the intensity

1 2 3 4 5 6 7 8 9 10

1 2 3 4 5 6 7 8 9 10

1 2 3 4 5 6 7 8 9 10

4   What thought patterns do you recognize?   (Circle any or write your own

All or nothing   Fortune telling   Minimizing the positive
Blaming others   Labeling   Overgeneralization
Catastrophizing   Magnifying the negative   Self-blaming
Emotional reasoning   Mind reading   Should statements

How can you think about the situation differently?   (Challenge your thoughts)

Make note of any additional reflections you have.

1   What happened?   (Describe the situation)

2   What is going through your mind?   (Describe the situation)

3   What emotions are you feeling?   (Note the intensity)

1 2 3 4 5 6 7 8 9 10

1 2 3 4 5 6 7 8 9 10

1 2 3 4 5 6 7 8 9 10

4   What thought patterns do you recognize?   (Circle any or write your own)

All or nothing   Fortune telling   Minimizing the positive
Blaming others   Labeling   Overgeneralization
Catastrophizing   Magnifying the negative   Self-blaming
Emotional reasoning   Mind reading   Should statements

How can you think about the situation differently?   (Challenge your thoughts)

Make note of any additional reflections you have.

1   What happened?   (Describe the situatio

. . . .

. . . .

. . . .

. . . .

. . . .

2   What is going through your mind?   (Describe the situatio

. . . .

. . . .

. . . .

. . . .

. . . .

3   What emotions are you feeling?   (Note the intensit

                                          1 2 3 4 5 6 7 8 9 1
. . . .
                                          1 2 3 4 5 6 7 8 9 1
. . . .
                                          1 2 3 4 5 6 7 8 9 1
. . . .

. . . .

. . . .

4   What thought patterns do you recognize?   (Circle any or write your ow

       All or nothing   Fortune telling   Minimizing the positiv
       Blaming others   Labeling   Overgeneralization
       Catastrophizing   Magnifying the negative   Self-blaming
       Emotional reasoning   Mind reading   Should statements

. . . .

. . . .

. . . .

. . . .

How can you think about the situation differently?   (Challenge your thoughts)

Make note of any additional reflections you have.

1   What happened?   (Describe the situatic

2   What is going through your mind?   (Describe the situatic

3   What emotions are you feeling?   (Note the intensi

1 2 3 4 5 6 7 8 9

1 2 3 4 5 6 7 8 9

1 2 3 4 5 6 7 8 9

4   What thought patterns do you recognize?   (Circle any or write your ow

All or nothing   Fortune telling   Minimizing the positi
Blaming others   Labeling   Overgeneralization
Catastrophizing   Magnifying the negative   Self-blaming
Emotional reasoning   Mind reading   Should statements

5   How can you think about the situation differently?   (Challenge your thoughts)

6   Make note of any additional reflections you have.

1   What happened?   (Describe the situation

2   What is going through your mind?   (Describe the situation

3   What emotions are you feeling?   (Note the intensity

1 2 3 4 5 6 7 8 9 10

1 2 3 4 5 6 7 8 9 10

1 2 3 4 5 6 7 8 9 10

4   What thought patterns do you recognize?   (Circle any or write your own

All or nothing	Fortune telling	Minimizing the positive
Blaming others	Labeling	Overgeneralization
Catastrophizing	Magnifying the negative	Self-blaming
Emotional reasoning	Mind reading	Should statements

How can you think about the situation differently?   (Challenge your thoughts)

Make note of any additional reflections you have.

1   What happened?   (Describe the situation)

2   What is going through your mind?   (Describe the situation)

3   What emotions are you feeling?   (Note the intensity)

1 2 3 4 5 6 7 8 9 10

1 2 3 4 5 6 7 8 9 10

1 2 3 4 5 6 7 8 9 10

4   What thought patterns do you recognize?   (Circle any or write your own)

All or nothing	Fortune telling	Minimizing the positive
Blaming others	Labeling	Overgeneralization
Catastrophizing	Magnifying the negative	Self-blaming
Emotional reasoning	Mind reading	Should statements

How can you think about the situation differently?   (Challenge your thoughts)

Make note of any additional reflections you have.

1   What happened?   (Describe the situatio

2   What is going through your mind?   (Describe the situatie

3   What emotions are you feeling?   (Note the intensi

                                             1 2 3 4 5 6 7 8 9
                                             1 2 3 4 5 6 7 8 9
                                             1 2 3 4 5 6 7 8 9

4   What thought patterns do you recognize?   (Circle any or write your ow

       All or nothing   Fortune telling   Minimizing the positi
       Blaming others   Labeling   Overgeneralization
       Catastrophizing   Magnifying the negative   Self-blaming
       Emotional reasoning   Mind reading   Should statements

How can you think about the situation differently?   (Challenge your thoughts)

Make note of any additional reflections you have.

1   What happened?   (Describe the situatio

2   What is going through your mind?   (Describe the situatio

3   What emotions are you feeling?   (Note the intensi

1 2 3 4 5 6 7 8 9

1 2 3 4 5 6 7 8 9

1 2 3 4 5 6 7 8 9

4   What thought patterns do you recognize?   (Circle any or write your ow

All or nothing   Fortune telling   Minimizing the positi
Blaming others   Labeling   Overgeneralization
Catastrophizing   Magnifying the negative   Self-blaming
Emotional reasoning   Mind reading   Should statements

How can you think about the situation differently?   (Challenge your thoughts)

Make note of any additional reflections you have.

1   What happened?   (Describe the situation

2   What is going through your mind?   (Describe the situation

3   What emotions are you feeling?   (Note the intensity

1 2 3 4 5 6 7 8 9 10

1 2 3 4 5 6 7 8 9 10

1 2 3 4 5 6 7 8 9 10

4   What thought patterns do you recognize?   (Circle any or write your own

All or nothing   Fortune telling   Minimizing the positive
Blaming others   Labeling   Overgeneralization
Catastrophizing   Magnifying the negative   Self-blaming
Emotional reasoning   Mind reading   Should statements

How can you think about the situation differently?   (Challenge your thoughts)

Make note of any additional reflections you have.

1   What happened?   (Describe the situation

2   What is going through your mind?   (Describe the situation

3   What emotions are you feeling?   (Note the intensity

1 2 3 4 5 6 7 8 9 10

1 2 3 4 5 6 7 8 9 10

1 2 3 4 5 6 7 8 9 10

4   What thought patterns do you recognize?   (Circle any or write your own

All or nothing   Fortune telling   Minimizing the positive
Blaming others   Labeling   Overgeneralization
Catastrophizing   Magnifying the negative   Self-blaming
Emotional reasoning   Mind reading   Should statements

How can you think about the situation differently?   (Challenge your thoughts)

Make note of any additional reflections you have.

1   What happened?   (Describe the situation

.   .   .   .

.   .   .   .

.   .   .   .

.   .   .   .

.   .   .   .

2   What is going through your mind?   (Describe the situation

.   .   .   .

.   .   .   .

.   .   .   .

.   .   .   .

.   .   .   .

3   What emotions are you feeling?   (Note the intensity

                                            1 2 3 4 5 6 7 8 9 1

                                            1 2 3 4 5 6 7 8 9 1

                                            1 2 3 4 5 6 7 8 9 1

.   .   .   .

.   .   .   .

4   What thought patterns do you recognize?   (Circle any or write your own

All or nothing	Fortune telling	Minimizing the positive
Blaming others	Labeling	Overgeneralization
Catastrophizing	Magnifying the negative	Self-blaming
Emotional reasoning	Mind reading	Should statements

.   .   .   .

.   .   .   .

.   .   .   .

.   .   .   .

.   .   .   .

How can you think about the situation differently?   (Challenge your thoughts)

Make note of any additional reflections you have.

1   What happened?   (Describe the situatio

2   What is going through your mind?   (Describe the situatio

3   What emotions are you feeling?   (Note the intensit

                                                1 2 3 4 5 6 7 8 9 1
                                                1 2 3 4 5 6 7 8 9 1
                                                1 2 3 4 5 6 7 8 9 1

4   What thought patterns do you recognize?   (Circle any or write your ow

        All or nothing   Fortune telling   Minimizing the positiv
        Blaming others   Labeling   Overgeneralization
        Catastrophizing   Magnifying the negative   Self-blaming
        Emotional reasoning   Mind reading   Should statements

How can you think about the situation differently?   (Challenge your thoughts)

Make note of any additional reflections you have.

1   What happened?   (Describe the situation

2   What is going through your mind?   (Describe the situation

3   What emotions are you feeling?   (Note the intensity

1 2 3 4 5 6 7 8 9 1

1 2 3 4 5 6 7 8 9 1

1 2 3 4 5 6 7 8 9 1

4   What thought patterns do you recognize?   (Circle any or write your own

All or nothing   Fortune telling   Minimizing the positive
Blaming others   Labeling   Overgeneralization
Catastrophizing   Magnifying the negative   Self-blaming
Emotional reasoning   Mind reading   Should statements

How can you think about the situation differently?   (Challenge your thoughts)

Make note of any additional reflections you have.

TOOL IV:
Growth Mindset

PRACTICE:
Reframing

Note From a Therapist

Growth Mindset is about the power that comes from believing change is possible. The slightest perspective shift towards hope can relieve some of the stress of feeling stuck.

This following exercise is about recognizing your ability to change and practicing flexible thinking. You'll be asked to take on the perspective of one of your close friends and consider how you would advise and support them. You might do this by acknowledging changes that have happened over time, recognizing how change is still possible, or identifying new approaches for growth in the future. You may end up recognizing skills and capabilities that you have now that you didn't have before (such as identifying feelings, or different reactions to triggers), or acknowledging that everyone makes mistakes and there's always an opportunity to grow or learn.

A note on self-compassion: We want to remind you that change is possible but also takes time. Be careful not to use growth mindset as another opportunity to beat yourself up. This activity can help you get comfortable with acknowledging strengths or changes that may be frequently overlooked or downplayed, as well as being kind with yourself about your ongoing development.

Adopting a growth mindset trains your brain to embrace the positive. You can learn more about Growth Mindset by going to Appendix G.

How to Approach This Section

How Often: Weekly, or more often as desired.

When: Anytime; can be especially helpful during
                difficult moments.

                When you notice yourself being critical,
                these exercises can be particularly helpful.
                Revisiting this often will help foster greater
                self-compassion and control in your
                day-to-day life.

Tips: It can be helpful to approach this section by
                taking a breath, and considering what you
                might say to a friend in the same situation.

                See if you can notice judgmental thoughts (i.e.
                "But that's not a big deal" or "I should have
                been able to do that") when they come up, and
                let yourself recognize accomplishment and
                growth anyway.

                If you've been trying something new that
                hasn't shown the changes you'd like, it may
                be time to take a break and consider a new
                strategy.

---

1   What happened or what thoughts are you having?

Instructions: Describe either a situation or some of the thoughts and feelings you're having.

Example: I've been feeling particularly sad and alone this weekend.

I sometimes feel this way but it feels worse than usual.

---

2   Now, imagine you're counseling a friend with the same thoughts.

2.1   How have things possibly improved since the past?

Instructions: Consider similar moments in the past. Compared to what they are thinking about currently, are there ways in which they have tried something new, shifted their attitude, or better accepted the current situation?

Example: You are much more aware of and willing to feel these difficult emotions. You use to be so hard on yourself for feeling down, but now it's a little easier and you don't feel the need to run away from these feelings.

2.2   How could they or the situation continue to change or improve?

Instructions: Reflect on what you've learned about growth mindset and describe some w in which things might change for the better.

Example: We know the brain continues to change. The way that you are being more accepting of your feelings is setting a new connection in your brain, and you're learning t those emotions aren't intolerable, or forever.

2.3   What are some things they can try differently in the future?

Instructions: Consider what you might brainstorm for your friend to try, or if there is a different approach to be considered. Naming even one small concrete step can be helpful.

Example: These feelings might be telling you that you could use some more connection in your life. I know that the feelings are still really hard, but maybe if you call a friend tomorro that'll help you feel differently, even if you still don't feel ideal.

Examples of
Helpful Reframing

_____ took a lot of effort to do

A while ago, this would have been nearly impossible for me

_____ is something I would like to be better at

I didn't do it as well as I might have liked, but that's okay

I tried _____ and some parts worked, and some didn't

I'm proud of myself for _____

I may not be very good at this now, but I will become better over time

Everybody has strengths and weaknesses. _____ is one of my strengths

I did _____ poorly, but that doesn't mean that I am a bad person or that I will always do it that way

I felt really worried and nervous about this going into it, and I'm grateful that it went alright

I am not perfect, and nobody ever is

_____ was an accomplishment today

I could try approaching this issue in the future differently by _____

I am striving to be better at _____ , and each day provides learning opportunities

1   What happened or what thoughts are you having?

2   Now, imagine you're counseling a friend with the same thoughts.

        2.1   How have things possibly improved since the past?

        2.2   How could they or the situation continue to change or improve?

        2.3   What are some things they can try differently in the future?

What happened or what thoughts are you having?

Now, imagine you're counseling a friend with the same thoughts.

    2.1   How have things possibly improved since the past?

    2.2   How could they or the situation continue to change or improve?

    2.3   What are some things they can try differently in the future?

1   What happened or what thoughts are you having?

2   Now, imagine you're counseling a friend with the same thoughts.

        2.1   How have things possibly improved since the past?

        2.2   How could they or the situation continue to change or improve?

        2.3   What are some things they can try differently in the future?

What happened or what thoughts are you having?

Now, imagine you're counseling a friend with the same thoughts.

2.1   How have things possibly improved since the past?

2.2   How could they or the situation continue to change or improve?

2.3   What are some things they can try differently in the future?

1   What happened or what thoughts are you having?

2   Now, imagine you're counseling a friend with the same thoughts.

     2.1   How have things possibly improved since the past?

     2.2   How could they or the situation continue to change or improve?

     2.3   What are some things they can try differently in the future?

What happened or what thoughts are you having?

Now, imagine you're counseling a friend with the same thoughts.

2.1   How have things possibly improved since the past?

2.2   How could they or the situation continue to change or improve?

2.3   What are some things they can try differently in the future?

1   What happened or what thoughts are you having?

2   Now, imagine you're counseling a friend with the same thoughts.

        2.1   How have things possibly improved since the past?

        2.2   How could they or the situation continue to change or improve?

        2.3   What are some things they can try differently in the future?

What happened or what thoughts are you having?

2   Now, imagine you're counseling a friend with the same thoughts.

   2.1   How have things possibly improved since the past?

   2.2   How could they or the situation continue to change or improve?

   2.3   What are some things they can try differently in the future?

1   What happened or what thoughts are you having?

2   Now, imagine you're counseling a friend with the same thoughts.

   2.1   How have things possibly improved since the past?

   2.2   How could they or the situation continue to change or improve?

   2.3   What are some things they can try differently in the future?

What happened or what thoughts are you having?

Now, imagine you're counseling a friend with the same thoughts.

2.1   How have things possibly improved since the past?

2.2   How could they or the situation continue to change or improve?

2.3   What are some things they can try differently in the future?

1   What happened or what thoughts are you having?

2   Now, imagine you're counseling a friend with the same thoughts.

    2.1   How have things possibly improved since the past?

    2.2   How could they or the situation continue to change or improve?

    2.3   What are some things they can try differently in the future?

What happened or what thoughts are you having?

Now, imagine you're counseling a friend with the same thoughts.

2.1   How have things possibly improved since the past?

2.2   How could they or the situation continue to change or improve?

2.3   What are some things they can try differently in the future?

1   What happened or what thoughts are you having?

2   Now, imagine you're counseling a friend with the same thoughts.

    2.1   How have things possibly improved since the past?

    2.2   How could they or the situation continue to change or improve?

    2.3   What are some things they can try differently in the future?

What happened or what thoughts are you having?

Now, imagine you're counseling a friend with the same thoughts.

2.1   How have things possibly improved since the past?

2.2   How could they or the situation continue to change or improve?

2.3   What are some things they can try differently in the future?

1   What happened or what thoughts are you having?

2   Now, imagine you're counseling a friend with the same thoughts.

     2.1   How have things possibly improved since the past?

     2.2   How could they or the situation continue to change or improve?

     2.3   What are some things they can try differently in the future?

What happened or what thoughts are you having?

2   Now, imagine you're counseling a friend with the same thoughts.

    2.1   How have things possibly improved since the past?

    2.2   How could they or the situation continue to change or improve?

    2.3   What are some things they can try differently in the future?

1   What happened or what thoughts are you having?

2   Now, imagine you're counseling a friend with the same thoughts.

2.1   How have things possibly improved since the past?

2.2   How could they or the situation continue to change or improve?

2.3   What are some things they can try differently in the future?

What happened or what thoughts are you having?

Now, imagine you're counseling a friend with the same thoughts.

2.1   How have things possibly improved since the past?

2.2   How could they or the situation continue to change or improve?

2.3   What are some things they can try differently in the future?

1   What happened or what thoughts are you having?

2   Now, imagine you're counseling a friend with the same thoughts.

    2.1   How have things possibly improved since the past?

    2.2   How could they or the situation continue to change or improve?

    2.3   What are some things they can try differently in the future?

What happened or what thoughts are you having?

Now, imagine you're counseling a friend with the same thoughts.

2.1   How have things possibly improved since the past?

2.2   How could they or the situation continue to change or improve?

2.3   What are some things they can try differently in the future?

TOOL V:
Dialectical Behavior Therapy and Interpersonal Effectiveness

PRACTICE: DEAR MAN

Note From a Therapist

Wherever we fall on the introverted-extroverted spectrum, we, like all mammals, are fundamentally social beings. But depression can interrupt our sociality, with thoughts like "you're too much," or "they don't like you." Those thoughts make it difficult to take care of yourself within relationships, make it hard to ask for what you need, and to assert your boundaries to create more balanced, positive, and stronger relationships. But when you are emotionally open, genuine, and vulnerable, you give the relationship an opportunity to grow, as well as foster a greater sense of connection.

DBT consists of four skills, but the following exercise covers the Interpersonal Effectiveness skill, which focuses on fostering more communicative and positive relationships. This highlighted skill helps you express your needs. It doesn't guarantee the other person will give you what you ask for, but it attempts to stop the guessing games.

"DEAR MAN" is an acronym that provides a framework for effectively asserting yourself without attacking the other person. The first portion (Describe, Express, Assert, Reinforce) will help you prepare a rough script for the conversation, while the latter portion (Mindful, Appear, Negotiate) will serve as a reminder for how to approach the conversation.

Interpersonal Effectiveness helps you set and hold boundaries. You can learn more about DBT by going to Appendix H.

How to Approach
This Section

How Often: As needed or weekly.

When: Anytime; can be especially helpful after
                  stressful interpersonal interactions. This
                  exercise provides a script outline for communi-
                  cating something you'd like to see change with
                  another person.

Tips: These entries are intended to help you plan
                  future conversations. These can be very logis-
                  tical ("cleaning the dishes after using them")
                  or more interaction oriented ("taking a couple
                  hours to cool off when getting into a heated
                  argument").

                  Rather than thinking only of stressful interac-
                  tions and relationships, try also thinking about
                  positive relationships you'd like to improve.

                  Be aware of when you present judgments or
                  thoughts as facts or feelings (i.e. "You were
                  being rude" or "I felt like you...")

                  When asserting your request, be as clear as
                  possible about the behavior you'd like to see.
                  Asking someone to "stop doing x" is a more
                  difficult request for them to accomplish than
                  "instead of x, please do y." Likewise, saying "I'd
                  like you to put away your dishes the same day
                  you use them" is more concrete than "I'd like
                  you to do a better job cleaning up."

Plan your script:

1   D   Describe the situation.

Instructions: What were the facts of the situation? Be careful to avoid judgments.

Example: You have asked me what I'd like to do or what I think we should do a few times now, but on several occasions, you've planned something else entirely and caught me by surprise.

2   E   Express your feelings about the situation.

Instructions: What feelings came up? Write them as "When this...I felt..."

Do not include thoughts in this section (e.g. "I felt that you were in the wrong").

Use the Feelings Wheel in Appendix A for help.

Example: When you planned a new event, I felt irritable and annoyed.

3   A   Assert yourself by asking for what you want.

Instructions: What did you want to see happen, precisely?

Example: I understand that you're gathering ideas, but I'd like it if you acknowledged my thoughts or told me you preferred an alternative, so it's not a surprise for me when our plans change.

4   R   Reinforce the reward.

Instructions: What benefits might the other person see? How might this improve the relationship?

Example: This way, I can know not to get attached to my ideas, or I can come up with plans I think we'll both enjoy.

When communicating this script, keep in mind the rest of the
DEAR MAN exercise:

M - Mindfully keep your focus on the objective. Maintain your
position and don't be distracted by other issues.

A - Appear confident. Aim for a confident tone and physical
manner; make good eye contact. Try to avoid stammering,
whispering, staring at the floor, retreating, and statements like
"I'm not sure," etc.

N - Negotiate by being willing to give in order to get. Offer
alternative solutions to the problem. Ask yourself, What am I
willing to "settle for" or "give up" in order to gain what I want in
this situation?

V	DEAR MAN	ENTRY 01		M	D	Y

1   D   Describe the situation.

2   E   Express your feelings about the situation.

3   A   Assert yourself by asking for what you want.

4   R   Reinforce the reward.

MAN   *Remember:* Mindfully keep your focus on the objective.
Appear Confident. Negotiate by being willing to give in order to get.

D   Describe the situation.

E   Express your feelings about the situation.

A   Assert yourself by asking for what you want.

R   Reinforce the reward.

MAN   *Remember:* Mindfully keep your focus on the objective.
           Appear Confident. Negotiate by being willing to give in order to get.

1   D   Describe the situation.

2   E   Express your feelings about the situation.

3   A   Assert yourself by asking for what you want.

4   R   Reinforce the reward.

MAN   *Remember:* Mindfully keep your focus on the objective.
        Appear Confident. Negotiate by being willing to give in order to get.

D   Describe the situation.

E   Express your feelings about the situation.

A   Assert yourself by asking for what you want.

R   Reinforce the reward.

MAN   *Remember:* Mindfully keep your focus on the objective.
         Appear Confident. Negotiate by being willing to give in order to get.

1   D   Describe the situation.

2   E   Express your feelings about the situation.

3   A   Assert yourself by asking for what you want.

4   R   Reinforce the reward.

MAN   *Remember:* Mindfully keep your focus on the objective.
Appear Confident. Negotiate by being willing to give in order to get.

D   Describe the situation.

E   Express your feelings about the situation.

A   Assert yourself by asking for what you want.

R   Reinforce the reward.

MAN   *Remember:* Mindfully keep your focus on the objective.
             Appear Confident. Negotiate by being willing to give in order to get.

1   D   Describe the situation.

2   E   Express your feelings about the situation.

3   A   Assert yourself by asking for what you want.

4   R   Reinforce the reward.

MAN   *Remember:* Mindfully keep your focus on the objective.
Appear Confident. Negotiate by being willing to give in order to get.

D   Describe the situation.

E   Express your feelings about the situation.

A   Assert yourself by asking for what you want.

R   Reinforce the reward.

MAN   *Remember:* Mindfully keep your focus on the objective.
         Appear Confident. Negotiate by being willing to give in order to get.

V	DEAR MAN	ENTRY 09	M	D	Y

1   D   Describe the situation.

. . . .

. . . .

. . . .

. . . .

. . . .

2   E   Express your feelings about the situation.

. . . .

. . . .

. . . .

. . . .

. . . .

3   A   Assert yourself by asking for what you want.

. . . .

. . . .

. . . .

. . . .

. . . .

4   R   Reinforce the reward.

. . . .

. . . .

. . . .

. . . .

MAN   *Remember:* Mindfully keep your focus on the objective.
Appear Confident. Negotiate by being willing to give in order to get.

D   Describe the situation.

E   Express your feelings about the situation.

A   Assert yourself by asking for what you want.

R   Reinforce the reward.

MAN   *Remember:* Mindfully keep your focus on the objective.
         Appear Confident. Negotiate by being willing to give in order to get.

1   D   Describe the situation.

. . . .

. . . .

. . . .

. . . .

. . . .

2   E   Express your feelings about the situation.

. . . .

. . . .

. . . .

. . . .

. . . .

3   A   Assert yourself by asking for what you want.

. . . .

. . . .

. . . .

. . . .

. . . .

4   R   Reinforce the reward.

. . . .

. . . .

. . . .

. . . .

. . . .

MAN   *Remember:* Mindfully keep your focus on the objective.
       Appear Confident. Negotiate by being willing to give in order to get.

D   Describe the situation.

E   Express your feelings about the situation.

A   Assert yourself by asking for what you want.

R   Reinforce the reward.

MAN   *Remember:* Mindfully keep your focus on the objective.
         Appear Confident. Negotiate by being willing to give in order to get.

1   D   Describe the situation.

. . . .

. . . .

. . . .

. . . .

. . . .

2   E   Express your feelings about the situation.

. . . .

. . . .

. . . .

. . . .

. . . .

3   A   Assert yourself by asking for what you want.

. . . .

. . . .

. . . .

. . . .

. . . .

4   R   Reinforce the reward.

. . . .

. . . .

. . . .

. . . .

. . . .

MAN   *Remember:* Mindfully keep your focus on the objective.
Appear Confident. Negotiate by being willing to give in order to get.

D   Describe the situation.

E   Express your feelings about the situation.

A   Assert yourself by asking for what you want.

R   Reinforce the reward.

MAN   *Remember:* Mindfully keep your focus on the objective.
           Appear Confident. Negotiate by being willing to give in order to get.

1   D   Describe the situation.

2   E   Express your feelings about the situation.

3   A   Assert yourself by asking for what you want.

4   R   Reinforce the reward.

MAN   *Remember:* Mindfully keep your focus on the objective.
           Appear Confident. Negotiate by being willing to give in order to get.

D   Describe the situation.

E   Express your feelings about the situation.

A   Assert yourself by asking for what you want.

R   Reinforce the reward.

MAN   *Remember:* Mindfully keep your focus on the objective.
           Appear Confident. Negotiate by being willing to give in order to get.

V	DEAR MAN	ENTRY 17	M	D	Y

1 D   Describe the situation.

· ·
· ·
· ·
· ·
· ·

2 E   Express your feelings about the situation.

· ·
· ·
· ·
· ·
· ·

3 A   Assert yourself by asking for what you want.

· ·
· ·
· ·
· ·
· ·

4 R   Reinforce the reward.

· ·
· ·
· ·
· ·

MAN   *Remember:* Mindfully keep your focus on the objective.
Appear Confident. Negotiate by being willing to give in order to get.

D   Describe the situation.

E   Express your feelings about the situation.

A   Assert yourself by asking for what you want.

R   Reinforce the reward.

MAN   *Remember:* Mindfully keep your focus on the objective.
         Appear Confident. Negotiate by being willing to give in order to get.

1   D   Describe the situation.

2   E   Express your feelings about the situation.

3   A   Assert yourself by asking for what you want.

4   R   Reinforce the reward.

MAN   *Remember:* Mindfully keep your focus on the objective.
        Appear Confident. Negotiate by being willing to give in order to get.

D   Describe the situation.

E   Express your feelings about the situation.

A   Assert yourself by asking for what you want.

R   Reinforce the reward.

MAN   *Remember:* Mindfully keep your focus on the objective.
         Appear Confident. Negotiate by being willing to give in order to get.

Final Note
From a Therapist

Congratulations. We recognize the determination and energy
required to finish this book and its exercises. Take a moment to
appreciate your work and persistence.

We've introduced a variety of tools and approaches, and
some may have resonated more than others. Take a moment to
consider which tools were most interesting, engaging, or useful
for you. Were there any that you felt particularly motivated by?
Any that gave you a sense of lightness or optimism?

We hope that this process of discovery and experimentation serves as a jumping off point for you—either through
repeating exercises in this book, diving deeper into particular
tools, or perhaps by seeking out a professional with experience in
the topics that resonated most deeply.

You can find our resource recommendations in Appendices A and C, and learn about other helpful tools in
Appendix B.

A   Helpful Resources
        I. The Feelings Wheel
        II. Cognitive Distortions

I.   THE FEELINGS WHEEL

In your journal entries, you are tasked with listing the
emotions you are feeling and rating their intensity.
Emotions are complex—finding the right words to
express them can be challenging but also very useful.
Describing that you are feeling "frustrated" or "jealous"
is more helpful than noting that you are feeling "bad" or
"anxious" because accurately describing your emotional
state will lead to an improved ability to understand,
communicate, and manage that emotional state.

The Feelings Wheel on the next page is a tool used
by therapists to help you quickly and accurately name the
emotions you are feeling. The wheel features three rings.
The innermost ring consists of six core emotions: joy, love,
fear, anger, sadness, and surprised. The outer two rings
include more detailed emotions associated with these core
emotions.

To use the Feelings Wheel, start by scanning all
three rings of the wheel for an emotion that resonates
with what you are feeling. Once you've identified that
emotion, you can move towards the center of the wheel
or away from the center to find the adjacent words that
most accurately reflect your feelings. For instance, you
might start with "sadness" and work outward to "guilty"
as a more accurate feeling. Alternatively, you might start
with "nervous" and work your way inward to "fear" and
then outward again to "insecure" because that feels more
accurate than "nervous."

The goal is not to end up at any particular ring of
the Feelings Wheel, though people do tend to gravitate
towards the outer rings of the wheel as they practice using
this tool. As you're getting started, simply focus on identifying and writing down the emotions that most clearly
reflect your emotional state.

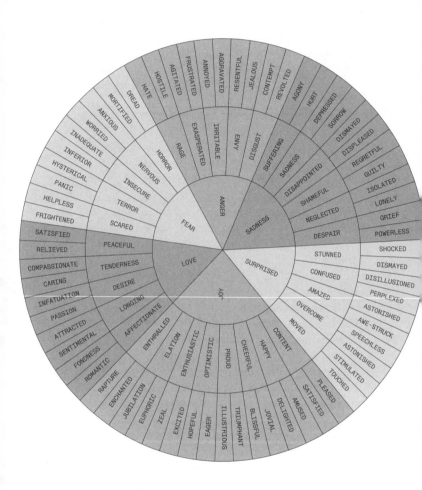

II.   COGNITIVE DISTORTIONS

Cognitive distortions are a set of automatic thought patterns that are inaccurate and reinforce negative thinking or emotions. These automatic negative thoughts "distort" our thinking by leading us to believe something that is both unhelpful and untrue.

Psychiatrist and researcher Aaron Beck is credited with first proposing the theory behind cognitive distortions in the 1970s; his student, David Burns, is credited with popularizing the common names of these distortions in the 1980s. In one of his books, Burns writes: "I suspect you will find that a great many of your negative feelings are in fact based on such thinking errors" given that our minds are predisposed to drawing connections between our thoughts and what we observe, it is likely that at least some of those connections are faulty and produce negative thinking.[5]

Cognitive distortions result in negative thinking and emotions, and therefore have a negative impact on our anxiety and well-being. By learning to identify and challenge these logical fallacies, as you are asked to do in the journal entries, you can develop more accurate and helpful thinking patterns over time.

In this journal, we've focused on 12 of the most common cognitive distortions, listed on the next page. Note that some of these cognitive distortions are similar or related—several can apply to any given situation.

1   ALL OR NOTHING THINKING

Sometimes called polarized or black-and-white thinking, this cognitive distortion leads you to perceive things at the extremes by removing the middle ground or room for mistakes. All or nothing thinking makes the assumption that there are only two possibilities in a given situation, often expressed in "either-or" terms. Based on your actions, you may think of yourself or others as being either great or awful, hard-working or lazy, delightful or intolerable.

Example:
"I ate ice cream today so I've ruined my diet completely."

Example of reframing:
"Even while dieting, I can have foods I enjoy purely for their taste."

2   BLAMING OTHERS

Unlike self-blaming, this cognitive distortion involves holding other people entirely accountable for a negative outcome. If a bad situation must be the fault of someone else, then you are other-blaming.

Example:
"Dinner got burned because Sam left the kitchen a mess and I couldn't find anything I needed."

Example of reframing:
"Sam left the kitchen a mess—I will talk to him about cleaning up after himself. But I could have also tidied up what space and things I needed before starting dinner."

3   CATASTROPHIZING

Catastrophizing is thinking about disastrous possibilities based on a relatively small observation or event; it can lead to believing that the worst case scenario is the one that will play out.

Example:
"I botched that part of the interview; they probably will go with someone more qualified than me. I'll never get a job in my field and my student debt will have been for nothing."

Example of reframing:
"I think I answered that question poorly in the interview, but I feel good about some other responses. Hopefully this works out, but I will still have options even if it doesn't."

4   EMOTIONAL REASONING

This distortion can be summed up as, "If I feel that way, it must be true." When engaged in emotional reasoning, you accept your emotional reaction as an automatic indicator of reality. In other words, emotional reasoning occurs when you believe that something is true because of your feelings about it.

Example:
"I feel angry. This waiter must be treating me unfairly."

Example of reframing:
"I've been feeling really tired and upset today because of a few things at work. I should probably take a walk or a few deep breaths."

5   FORTUNE TELLING

Similar to mind reading, fortune telling refers to making dramatic predictions about the future with little or no evidence. Just as mind-reading overestimates our ability to know what other people are thinking, fortune-telling overestimates our ability to know what will happen in the future.

Example:
"The last relationship only lasted 2 months...this one probably will too."

Example of reframing:
"I'm going to do my best to do what I feel is right for this new relationship, regardless of how long it lasts."

6   LABELING

This cognitive distortion is an extension of overgeneralization that involves assigning negative global judgment (i.e., about an entire person or thing) based on a small amount of evidence. These labels create inaccurate views of the people, places, and things around us.

Example:
"I sent the invite to the wrong person. I'm so stupid."

Example of reframing:
"Ugh, I made a mistake and sent the invite to the wrong person. I feel pretty embarrassed."

7   MAGNIFYING THE NEGATIVE

Also referred to as filtering or tunnel vision, magnifying the negative fixates our thoughts on only the negative parts of a situation. By dwelling on the negative, our fears, losses, and irritations become exaggerated in importance and the positive parts of the situation not given fair consideration.

Example:
"I can't believe I included a typo in my email to HR, they are definitely going to reject my request."

Example of reframing:
"I had a typo in my email to HR, but my meaning is still clear."

8   MIND READING

Mind reading involves making assumptions about what others are thinking and feeling based on limited evidence. Though it is possible to have an idea of what others are thinking, these intuitions are often inaccurate because there are so many factors that influence the thoughts and feelings of others that we are not aware of.

Example:
"The cashier must think I'm some weirdo for wearing this outfit to the store."

Example of reframing:
"I feel a bit self-conscious of my outfit, but others may not notice or care."

9   MINIMIZING THE POSITIVE

Whereas magnifying the negative turns up the volume on anything bad, minimizing the positive actively reduces the volume of anything good. Specifically, this means ignoring the value or importance of the positive parts of a situation.

Example:
"Anybody could have done what I did, they're just being nice to compliment me for it."

Example of reframing:
"I did something that people find valuable and praise-worthy."

10   OVERGENERALIZATION

In overgeneralization, you draw broad conclusions based on just one piece of evidence. This thought pattern is often based on the assumption that one bad experience means that whenever you're in a similar situation, the bad experience will repeat itself. You can often identify overgeneralizations by looking for words that imply absolutes such as "all," "none," "never," and "always."

Example:
"I always get nervous and screw up presentations."

Example of reframing:
"Presentations tend to make me feel nervous."

11 SELF-BLAMING

Sometimes known as personalization, this distortion involves believing that you are entirely responsible for a negative situation, even for factors that are outside of your control. Self-blaming also often assumes that what other people do or say is a reaction to you.

Example:
"I was late to hanging out with my friend and ruined what would've otherwise been a good time."

Example of reframing:
"I wish I hadn't been late, but it happens sometimes and I'm not fully responsible for how she felt."

12 SHOULD STATEMENTS

Should statements involve creating narrow and inflexible rules about how you and other people should behave. Specifically, it means believing that you or other people "should" or "must" act a certain way and if they do not, they are judged as faulty or wrong in some way. This distortion imposes a set of expectations that will very likely not be met; you feel guilty when you break them and angry when others break them.

Example:
"I shouldn't have been so upset with her. I should have been more calm and understanding."

Example of reframing:
"It's understandable that I felt hurt and it is helpful to communicate that. Next time, I can try to approach the situation more calmly."

B   Fundamentals of Self-Care

Working through the fundamentals of self-care can give you some initial momentum into doing the work of learning new skills and tools, and can often immediately improve how you feel. Listed below are various domains of foundational self-care and some ideas of things to do. You may have already learned many of these, but reminders are helpful. This is a checklist many clinicians will begin with.

NUTRITION

Maintaining your body's nutritional needs is essential for regulating your mood. Even if you think you can work through to the next meal, your ability to think, communicate effectively, and manage your emotions are impaired.

Try to feed yourself through-out the day (three or more snacks or meals is a good start), doing your best to include a variety of food groups.

EXERCISE

Movement releases endorphins, which in turn relieves stress. Give yourself permission to turn up your favorite song and let your body guide you.

Try stretching while watching TV, or walking around the block when you want to clear your head.

SUBSTANCE USE

Caffeine, alcohol, cannabis, and other substances can disrupt your ability to experience and regulate your emotions. Be aware of excessive or unhelpful use.

A way to limit substances is to buy less to decrease its availability, and to put it in inconvenient places (e.g. above the fridge, or in the back of a closet) to make it harder to access.

PHYSICAL HEALTH

Illnesses, chronic issues, and hormonal imbalances can take a toll on your mental health and sometimes mimic the symptoms of certain disorders (some estimate 5-10% of depression patients are undiagnosed cases of hypothyroidism).[28]

Make regular check-ups a priority, and be sure to speak to your doctor about any depressive symptoms.

SLEEP

Sufficient quantity (7-9 hours for most) and quality of sleep are both important. Studies continue to show how sufficient sleep directly improves the brain's ability to regulate emotions and keep mood and anxiety levels from worsening.[24]

Try to use your bed only for sleep and keep a regular bedtime. Set up a corner of the room with fluffy blankets and pillows as an alternative spot to be comfortable instead of lounging in bed.

MINDFULNESS

Over the past decade, research has shown that mindfulness practices may physically increase the size of brain regions associated with regulating emotion.[29] Mindfulness, the practice of being nonjudgmentally aware of the present moment, is now regularly used by clinicians to help with symptoms of anxiety and depression.

Take a moment to name five things you see, four things you touch, three sounds, two smells, and one taste. Finish by taking one really deep breath.

SOCIAL CONNECTION

Quality social relationships have been shown to improve lifespan and reduce risk for heart disease among many other physical and mental health benefits.[30] It can also help to start by finding small ways to feel less isolated: for instance sharing with or contributing to others in any way (share how you are feeling or share a funny meme).

Ask someone how they're doing today, or pay them a small compliment.

C   Additional Resources

If you'd like to dive deeper into any of the topics and tools in the book, we wanted to offer at least a few trustworthy resources to explore further (this is by no means an exhaustive list).

ON DEPRESSION

Book: *The Noonday Demon: An Atlas of Depression* by A. Solomon

ACCEPTANCE AND COMMITMENT THERAPY

Books: *The Happiness Trap* by R. Harris, or *Get Out of Your Mind and into Your Life* by S. Smith and S. Hayes.
Podcast: ACT in Context
Web: https://www.actmindfully.com.au/free-stuff/

BEHAVIORAL ACTIVATION

Book: *Overcoming Depression One Step at a Time: The New Behavioral Activation Approach to Getting Your Life Back* by M. Addis and C. Martell

COGNITIVE BEHAVIORAL THERAPY

Book: *Feeling Good* by David Burns
Podcast: *Feeling Good Podcast*

GROWTH MINDSET

Book: *Mindset* by Carol Dweck

DIALECTICAL BEHAVIOR THERAPY

Book: *Dialectical Behavior Therapy Skills Workbook* by M. McKay,
J. Wood, & J. Brantley
Web: https://www.dialecticalbehaviortherapy.com

OTHER

Many clinician-trusted worksheets can be found here for free:
https://www.therapistaid.com/

D   *Learn:* Acceptance and Commitment Therapy

TURNING PAIN INTO PURPOSE

Pain is uncomfortable. It stings and grates, burns and aches. And that's just physical pain: emotional wounds can be just as difficult to bear. For some, emotional pain can actually be more intense than physical pain.[31] So it's understandable that we go to such great lengths to avoid facing difficult emotions. We minimize our sadness, deny our anger, and distract ourselves from grief. But this relief is almost always temporary, and trying to maintain it doesn't always help us feel better. In fact, the effort it takes to suppress our pain can actually end up making it worse.

That's the particularly sticky problem Acceptance and Commitment Therapy (ACT, pronounced "act") tries to tackle. This evidence-based treatment takes a counterintuitive approach: it urges us to turn towards the pain. By accepting the pain that will inevitably come our way, we can build the life we want, without needing to wait to act until we feel better. Rather than trying to control or change our feelings, ACT urges us to redirect our energy towards positive actions that give us a greater sense of purpose. We can show up now, as we are, and simply act with intention.

THE EVIDENCE

Many of the first behavioral treatments for anxiety and depression focused on challenging painful thoughts through reason and logic. But as Dr. Steven Hayes, the creator of ACT says, "feeling good can be a very unhappy pursuit."[32] He developed ACT in the 1980s by combining traditional Cognitive Behavioral Therapy (CBT) techniques with Buddhist and other spiritual philosophies, which focus not on eliminating difficult emotions, but on accepting them for what they are: natural, understandable, and temporary. ACT has become increasingly popular since its development, with growing evidence that supports its efficacy and willingness to take a different approach than traditional treatments. One 2015 review of 39 trials found that ACT was as effective in treating anxiety and depression as traditional CBT.[33]

ACT is part of what some practitioners call the "third wave" of behavioural therapies, all of which emphasize mindfulness as a key component of treatment. Mindfulness, which has become something of a buzzword, is essentially the practice of tuning into the present moment. It is an incredibly powerful tool: numerous studies have shown that mindfulness therapy decreases the size of the amygdala, a brain region linked with emotional reactivity, and increases the size of the prefrontal cortex and hippocampus, regions linked to emotional regulation and memory.[34][35][36] What these studies (and others like it) show is that there is a strong biological basis for the ability of ACT to create positive change and relieve depression.

PSYCHOLOGICAL FLEXIBILITY & THE SIX CORE PRINCIPLES

When confronted with a difficult situation or an experience that causes emotional pain, it is understandable that our first instinct is to recoil from it. We might think "I can't handle this any longer," or "This hurts too much!" Humans, after all, are wired for survival. What ACT suggests is that this reaction, however natural, can actually disrupt our ability to process or move through painful emotions. Simply accepting how we feel, instead of suppressing our emotions, has been shown to measurably improve heart rate and mood.[37]

This ability—to be fully present with our feelings, and to navigate through difficult situations as they arise—is known as psychological flexibility. The main goal of ACT is to build this muscle, which it does through six core principles:

- Contact with the Present Moment (also called mindfulness)
- Acceptance
- Defusion
- The Observing Self
- Values
- Committed Action

Imagine you've been putting off a project, now due tomorrow. By engaging in *contact with the present moment*, you may notice your hands on the keyboard, a heavy dread in your chest, and a torrent of spiralling thoughts: "I don't know what I'm doing. Why can't I just get this over with? Something is seriously wrong with me." It's easy to drown in this swell of self-recrimination, but ACT encourages activating the observing self. From a place of neutral observation, we can recognize ourselves having these thoughts and feelings as though we were seeing it play out on a screen.

When we remove ourselves from our internal dialogue and observe our thoughts without reacting, we practice defusion. The thought, "Something is seriously wrong with me," is really no different, biologically speaking, than "What a cute puppy!" Both are the result of neurons firing in the brain. ACT teaches us that we don't need to do anything with our thoughts, such as evaluate their veracity or provide counter arguments. We don't need to fight our thoughts, and by practicing acceptance of the situation and our reaction, we can hold these thoughts with a lighter grip. It is normal to feel anxious before a highly antici-pated task; our brain doesn't have to also work overtime to try to "fix" unwanted sensations.

Once we accept we don't need to control our internal experiences, we can redirect our energy towards committed actions that we choose with intention, based on our values. Our values represent the way we want to be in the world—in this example, our desire to be recognized for our dependability and intelligence. Rather than procrastinating by scrolling through social media, you can act according to your values by acknowl-edging and accepting your dread, and still setting a timer for an intentional thirty-minute work session.

LIVING A PURPOSEFUL LIFE

ACT reminds us that there is no such thing as a life without pain. We feel deeply because we care deeply. And building an inten-tional life that celebrates your core values comes with a measure of discomfort. We expose ourselves to the possibility of success, failure, vulnerability, and connection. ACT urges us to greet the inherent pain and joy of being human with openness as we create a life rich with meaningful purpose.

E   *Learn:* Behavioral Activation

DOING THINGS

Depression is a sticky, muddy, cycle of reinforcement. We feel bad, so we do less. The less we do, the worse we feel. We sink further into the couch. We screen phone calls. We tell ourselves we'll do it when we feel better, but tomorrow comes and goes, and now we feel even worse. This is one of depression's cruelest tricks. Thankfully, there's an intuitive way to break this cycle. Behavioral Activation (BA) is an evidence-based treatment with a simple premise: take action first, and feel better later.

We tend to believe that we need to feel like doing something before doing it—that we should see friends only when we feel social, or run errands only when we feel motivated. BA teaches us that our actions can come before our emotions. When we engage in a new behavior, no matter how small, we build momentum. Motivation builds on motivation, and the more energized we feel, the more we do. These tiny actions are proven to shift our mood, which is why BA is often one of the first lines of defense for even severe depression. It may seem impossibly, even annoyingly, simple, but study after study confirms that doing the thing can truly make you feel better.[38][39] So call your friend, take the walk around the block, crack open that new book—just begin. The motivation, we promise, will follow.

THE EVIDENCE

Behavioral Activation was first introduced in the 1970s by Dr. Peter Lewinsohn. With its innovative approach prioritizing simple, manageable goals, it has become one of the most established and trusted tools for depression.

The American Psychological Association recognized BA as an evidence-based treatment for depression in the 1990s, with one landmark study showing it reduced depression just as meaningfully as Cognitive Behavioral Therapy.[40] Dozens of randomized control trials and meta-analysis consistently support its efficacy, and its simplicity and effectiveness means it is nearly always included in standard treatment plans.[41]

Moreover, BA can actually change how your brain functions. In one study, people with major depression who were treated with BA showed increased activity in their striatum, a region of the brain critical to motivation.[42]

THE CORE: TRACKING, PLANNING, DOING

A therapist using Behavioral Activation may begin by asking you to track your daily activities and moods. It's important to acknowledge that, while simple, this can also be daunting. Depression drops a scrim over your days. Seeing our perceived "failures" on the page can feel overwhelming, but there is true value here: While it is easy to focus on the low points, you can also look for moments when you felt a brief uptick in your mood, or more comfort in your body. This level of removal serves a purpose: when you can look at your daily life from a distance, you'll be able to identify important links between your behavior and your emotions.

JOY AND ACHIEVEMENT

Depression will try to convince you of the futility of taking action. It will tell you you're too tired, it's too hard, or there's no point. But each individual activity, and the resulting chemicals your brain and body release, helps rewrite the story. After taking stock of your daily rhythms, a clinician might ask you to add one small activity to your day. This could be listening to a podcast, playing the guitar for 10 minutes, or walking to the park—anything that may give you a sense of pleasure and achievement. They will help you draw a distinction between behaviors that are enjoyable in the moment—scrolling social media, mindlessly eating potato chips—and those that combine enjoyment with accomplishment. Try asking yourself: What did I used to enjoy doing? What brought me joy? If I weren't feeling this way, what would I be doing? And remind yourself: this will get easier. Over time, you'll be able to more clearly recognize what boosts your mood, and gravitate to those activities more often.

SPECIFIC, MANAGEABLE PLANS

Start small. Take each action and break it into its component parts. If you want to exercise in the morning, lay out your clothes the night before, and keep your phone in another room so you won't get distracted. Remember to approach the process like an experiment: you want to test what might happen to your mood and sense of accomplishment if you do things your brain might assume will have no effect. Behavioral Activation is as much about setting goals as it is addressing the barriers to those goals. If your plan doesn't work out, you can always adjust. Sometimes we need to pace ourselves or reassess our expectations of what we can accomplish in a given day. Each step we take towards action is worth celebrating.

DOING THE HARD THINGS

While early forms of BA focused exclusively on increasing pleasant activities, the approach has come to include all activities, both enjoyable and difficult, that add value to our lives. Take doing the dishes. As the pile of dirty dishes grows in the sink, we become more avoidant. BA works because it is practical and pragmatic: we can learn to do routine tasks without needing to create a story around them. We recognize the dishes for what they are—just dishes—rather than an emblem of our failure. By leaning into the discomfort of an activity, we increase the attendant sense of accomplishment on the other side. We learn that taking action is a lot less painful than we built it up to be.

ONE ACTIVITY A DAY

The simplicity of Behavioral Activation is why some still regard it both with curiosity and skepticism, yet the research continues to show just how effective it is. Just one action a day can lead to much bigger changes. As difficult as it might be to start, the simplest, smallest act can make a difference. In time, taking that first step—out of the darkness, out of bed, and into the world— will feel easier and easier, allowing you to stay engaged in, and optimistic about, your life.

F *Learn:* Cognitive Behavioral Therapy

THINK DIFFERENT, FEEL DIFFERENT

Our thoughts are how we engage with our world. They are how we understand, interpret, and assess; they are also how we conceptualize who we are and what our purpose is. It's no wonder that we become so deeply attached to what we think, so entrenched in certain patterns or beliefs.

And yet thoughts are not reality: they are, instead, the way we process reality. The same experience can be entirely different, depending on our interpretation. Construction noise outside could be a minor nuisance, or it could ruin our day. We may not even be aware of the process, but our thoughts, and the feelings they give rise to, inform our experience of the world.

The more we tune into our thoughts, the more we may notice that our mind follows certain patterns, or spirals down the same, well-trodden paths. Unfortunately, when we're feeling depressed, these patterns and paths are often extremely unhelpful. They also feel inescapable. This is why David Burns, one of the psychiatrists credited for popularizing Cognitive Behavioral Therapy (CBT), calls depression a "powerful form of mental black magic."[5] We can become convinced that our negative thoughts are our reality.

CBT, the leading evidence-based treatment for depression, asserts that it is our thoughts—and not our reality—that is causing our negative states. If we want to change how we feel, it says, then we have to change how we think. Using proven and practical tools, CBT helps individuals examine their thoughts, challenge their veracity, and, if necessary, form new patterns of thinking.

THE EVIDENCE FOR CBT

The 1950s and 60s ushered in a seismic shift in the field of modern psychotherapy, as practitioners moved away from Freudian psychoanalysis and embraced more scientifically testable methods of treatment. Through rigorous, evidence-based research, the founders of CBT—Dr. Albert Ellis and Dr. Aaron Beck—developed a framework that looked at the connections between our thoughts, feelings, and behaviors, helping patients observe and change thought patterns that cause negative emotions. CBT is now considered the "gold standard" treatment for depression and is the single most well-researched form of psychotherapy.[43] According to the National Institutes of Health, American Psychological Association, and other international guidelines, CBT is the first-line treatment for depression and many other mental health diagnoses, and has laid the foundation for numerous evidence-based treatments, including those discussed throughout this notebook.

THE ABC CHAIN

CBT reminds us that while we may not have control over what happens to us, we do have control over how we react. The "ABC" model in CBT explains how our thinking impacts our perception of an event, which leads to an emotional response:

- Activating event
- Belief
- Consequence

Here, the activating event (a situation) triggers a belief (a thought) which leads to a consequence (a feeling). The activating event does not inherently carry emotional weight, but the way we make sense of it is what creates our feelings. Let's take an example. Imagine you arrive at your coffee shop just as it is closing, and the employee won't let you in. You may think, "How dare he, he clearly has it out for me," or "It's all my fault, I shouldn't have come so late."

These are different interpretations of the same event, but both cause negative emotions: in this case, anger and disappointment. One of the core practices of CBT is to notice the ABC chain and challenge our unhelpful thoughts. When we disrupt irrational beliefs and replace them with more rational ones, we have healthier emotional responses. We come to realize that events are not further evidence of our bad luck or unworthiness. Instead, we can replace our negative thoughts with more helpful ones: "That's frustrating, but I can come back tomorrow," or "At least I got to take a walk." It's a subtle shift, but the impact can be tremendous.

FEEDBACK LOOP

How we think affects how we feel, which in turn impacts how we act. But this chain of events doesn't only move in one direction. Our thoughts, feelings, and behaviors exist in a feedback loop. Take the previous example. Having an aggressive, annoyed reaction to the coffee shop being closed might make us feel defensive, which could stir up more negative thoughts ("I can't do anything right!"), making us feel even worse. These feedback loops happen quickly, provoking intense feelings that are far removed from the situation itself. Our body reacts to the feedback loop: our heart rate increases, our muscles tense, we sweat, and breath becomes rapid and shallow. But with practice, we might notice the loop we're in, take a few deep breaths, and pause to question the validity of our thoughts. We can ask ourselves, "Is there another way I can think about this situation?"

AUTOMATIC THOUGHTS
AND COGNITIVE DISTORTIONS

Our minds are a constant parade of thoughts, many of which we are not even aware of. CBT calls these quick, unconscious thoughts "automatic thoughts," which arise without intention but can have an outsized impact on how we feel and act. We tend to take these automatic thoughts at face value. But our brains often take the fastest route possible to a conclusion, which may filter information through a lens and lead to unhelpful patterns that CBT practitioners term "cognitive distortions." These distortions, which are inherently biased and can reinforce negative patterns, can have a negative impact on our mental health. However, they can also be overcome.

Below are a few of the most common cognitive distortions that occur with depression. Every time you notice a cognitive distortion, you can ask yourself, "Is there an alternative way I could interpret this event?" This is called "reframing," which can help you replace unhelpful thinking patterns with more helpful ones.

ALL OR NOTHING THINKING

All or nothing thinking or black-or-white thinking, happens when we see things in extremes. Things are either "good" or "bad"; you can only "win" or "fail." We can counter these thoughts with interpretations that allow for more of a spectrum.

Example: "I forgot my friend's birthday, I'm a terrible friend!"

Reframe: "Even good friends can make mistakes. I show up for my friends in other meaningful ways."

EMOTIONAL REASONING

Emotional reasoning is interpreting reality based on our emotions. In short, "If I feel this way, it must be true." With practice, we can accept we feel a certain way, without taking it as factual proof of a situation.

Example: "I feel so sad and hopeless. I'm never going to get better."

Reframe: "Even though I feel really terrible right now, that doesn't mean I will always feel bad. I've felt this way in the past and gotten through it."

MINIMIZING THE POSITIVE

Minimizing the positive is ignoring or downplaying the positive aspects of a situation. Conversely, we can also dwell on the negative. By reevaluating, we can learn to give all facets of a situation fair consideration.

Example: "The only thing I did today was buy groceries."

Reframe: "I took care of myself today by leaving the house to get the food I need. I also brushed my teeth, washed my face, did the dishes, and took time for myself."

CHANGE YOUR THOUGHTS TO CHANGE HOW YOU FEEL

Being prone to this kind of distorted thinking does not mean you are a flawed person; it just means your thinking style is not serving you. No matter the strength or persistence of your negative thoughts, CBT can help. Your thoughts can become a pathway to feeling good.

As you begin to understand the connection between your thoughts and your feelings, you notice where you have a choice. Each time you interpret a situation in a negative way—and, by consequence, feel badly—you can challenge the underlying thought. The more you practice, the more automatic these helpful thinking patterns will become. Soon enough, you'll be able to experience life without the filter of your cognitive distortions, your reality will become clearer, and you will feel better.

G   *Learn:* Growth Mindset

CHANGE IS POSSIBLE

Receiving a diagnosis of depression—or simply coming to recognize your symptoms—can be a step towards finding relief, but sometimes, the label itself feels like an inherent part of our identity. Maybe you've tried multiple treatments, or made adjustments to your routines and schedules, and still feel like you can't gain any clarity or momentum. But having the sense that you are beyond hope is an illusion of depression. Everyone is capable of change.

In the past few decades, we have learned two critical things about mental health: first, that even the brain changes constantly, and second, that believing that this change is possible can actually make you feel better. Believing in your own potential for growth is what psychologists call a "growth mindset."

Even if you are not predisposed to a growth mindset, your beliefs about yourself can change, too. A slight shift in your understanding of your development can have a profoundly positive impact on your life. Through conscious effort, anyone can adopt a growth mindset and stretch beyond what they thought possible.

EVIDENCE

To fully grasp the value of growth mindset as a tool for depression, it is important to understand two concepts: first, that change is possible—as in, the brain is changing, and your efforts can affect this change; and second, that simply believing in your innate ability to change actually improves symptoms of depression.

The understanding that the brain undergoes continual change was not always a given. In fact, for most of the 20th century, scientists believed that the brain developed through childhood into its final, fixed adult state. However, scientists have since discovered that the brain continues to change on a daily basis. By studying the neurons of snail slugs, Nobel laureate Eric Kandel discovered specific molecular pathways that cause neuron connections to strengthen over time as they are used, and weaken when they are not.[44]

When a pathway is repeatedly stimulated, specific genes within neurons help foster connections between cells and make those cells more sensitive to stimuli in the future.

When a pathway is used less frequently, connections begin to decay. This is your brain's version of the "use it or lose it" principle; or, in neuroscience terms, "neurons that fire together, wire together." Every stimulation, thought, or event leads to a chemical change in the brain, and some changes, when repeated, can last longer than others.

The brain's ability and inclination towards change is known as neuroplasticity. New brain cells are being created daily, different connections are constantly rearranging, and we now know these changes occur right until the end of our lives.[45] It is a powerful reminder of our resilience and that change is possible. Psychologists have discovered that simply understanding our own propensity for change—what is known as "growth mindset"—can make us feel more satisfied and less stressed. In certain studies, teaching a growth mindset to healthy populations protects against anxiety and depression, and in depressed patients it actually reduces symptoms.[46][47] One groundbreaking study showed that just a single session produced impressive results.[48] Students were taught how the brain can change, given testimonials, and provided a few exercises to practice what they had learned. After just 30 minutes, symptoms of depression significantly decreased and the effects lasted at least nine months.

GROWTH VS. FIXED MINDSET
AND PERCEIVED CONTROL

If you have a growth mindset, you believe that you can improve. You view failure as a chance to learn, criticism as helpful, and challenges as part of a journey of continued improvement. If you have a fixed mindset, you believe that your qualities are unchangeable. You see failure as permanent, criticism as a personal attack, and challenges as something to avoid. These states, of course, are not definite, nor do they necessarily apply across all areas of your life. You might be open to experimentation and practice as a cook, but feel that the state of believing you will improve in time, your mental health will never change no matter what you try. But adopting a growth mindset as it applies to your mental health empowers you to understand that every time you sit with a hard feeling or challenge an unhelpful thought, you are disrupting old patterns and moving towards recovery.

In fact, having a growth mindset can build your sense of what experimental psychologists call "perceived control"—the opposite of a sense of powerlessness. Some psychologists believe that depression is essentially "learned helplessness": in other words, the culmination of stressful or traumatic life events, and the belief that the outcome of these events is somehow preordained.[49][50] Yet this belief is another one of depression's tricks. While we cannot always control what happens to us, we can control how we respond; and, in many cases, our responses are as significant as the events themselves. As one study demonstrated, there is a positive correlation between improved perceived control and improved depression symptoms.[48] This same study showed that adopting a growth mindset significantly improves an individual's sense of perceived control.

"THE POWER OF YET"

When recovering from depression, any regression can feel like it sends us back to square one. Maybe you felt caught in the undertow of heavy emotions and engaged in unhealthy habits. Maintaining "the power of yet," as Dweck calls it, means recognizing these moments as opportunities for growth rather than evidence we are backsliding. You can zoom out and identify ways that you are making progress. Yes, you had a difficult night, but maybe these moments are getting less frequent and less potent, and you have more awareness of what's happening in the moment. You can investigate factors that led to this unhelpful coping strategy. Maybe you needed to eat something, or overextended yourself during the day. You can brainstorm healthier coping strategies for the next time, like calling a friend or watching a funny movie. By putting yourself in a growth mindset, you will start to view perceived "failures" as feedback, and praise the efforts you make in your healing process.

GROWTH THROUGH COMPASSION

Many of us believe that we need to keep ourselves on a tight leash in order to improve. We criticize and punish in a way we never would with a friend, to whom we extend compassion and empathy. Yet research shows that self-criticism is highly ineffective in personal development: it worsens your mood and decreases your sense of hope.[51] Self-compassion, on the other hand, consistently correlates with fewer symptoms of depression.[52][53][54] Resist the urge to criticize yourself for, well, criticizing yourself—simply becoming aware of your mindset means you're closer to changing it. Next time, you can meet yourself where you are, without judgment, and gently redirect your self-recrimination towards compassionate understanding.

THE POSSIBILITY OF CHANGE

The idea that a simple shift in understanding your own ability to change might sound like a recipe for false hope. But your mindset is merely a set of conclusions you have about yourself and the world. The qualities you think are innate are not set in stone. Science has proven that we are capable of profound growth, and adopting a growth mindset towards your own mental health—while requiring a bit of a leap of faith—is a measurable step towards feeling better.

H   *Learn:* Dialectical Behavior Therapy and Interpersonal Effectiveness

EMOTION REGULATION AND RELATIONSHIPS

Humans are social creatures. Our relationships—with friends, family, and partners—give our lives meaning. Perhaps understandably, then, they can also be the source of our greatest friction and emotional distress. We know that positive relationships boost our mood, and that difficult ones can compound stress over time. So how do we balance our very human need for connection with the inevitable conflicts that arise from our most intense and meaningful relationships?

This understanding—that our relationships are necessary sources of joy and that maintaining them is key to overall happiness—forms the basis of many skills and modalities used in treatments for depression. Dialectical Behavioral Therapy (DBT) is a skills-based treatment that helps you to cope with difficult emotions, particularly those triggered in connection to others.

EVIDENCE

Along with ACT, DBT is also part of the "third wave" of therapies derived from the principles that led to CBT.[55] However, DBT is unique in that it was originally created to treat populations with very intense emotions and self-harming tendencies.[56] The creator of DBT, Dr. Marsha Linehan, spent much of her teens and early adulthood in and out of psychiatric hospitals for severe self-injurious behavior. Her commitment to helping people like her culminated in an evidence-based therapy that combines CBT and mindfulness practices. This comprehensive treatment was initially designed for patients with Borderline Personality Disorder, but has since been shown to be effective for many issues, including aggression, substance abuse, eating disorders, trauma, and depression.[57][58]

DBT is a well-respected approach among clinicians because it deeply understands the needs of people that are suffering and offers four specific skills to help them cope. The most traditional form of DBT has a 24 week duration: patients focus on 6 weeks per skill, with individual one-on-one sessions, group-sessions to practice skills, phone-coaching, and homework. Individual DBT skills have also been shown to be effective on their own. [59] Mindfulness, a core aspect of DBT, has been found to be effective at reducing the risk of having another major depressive episode.

WALKING THE MIDDLE

"Dialectical" means holding two opposing truths at the same time.[60] We tend to think of our world in black and white; when one feeling seems to invalidate another, it seems impossible that both things could be true. And yet humans are uniquely capable of containing seemingly opposing emotions, like gratitude and resentment, trust and fear, desire and disgust. DBT encourages us to see things as "both and," rather than "either or." It was this shortcoming of traditional treatments that Linehan focused on when developing DBT.

Treatments that told patients they needed to change their behaviors and feelings made people feel criticized and small, while treatments that told patients to accept themselves as they were invalidated the extent of their suffering and need for change. DBT teaches us that we can both have the desire to change our current reality, and be willing to accept the present moment for what it is. Thinking dialectically also applies to our relationships. We can love someone and accept that they have disappointed us; be angry and understand that the relationship can withstand conflict.

THE FOUR SKILLS

MINDFULNESS

As in many of the tools discussed in this workbook, mindfulness plays a key role in DBT. While the concept of mindfulness may sometimes feel inscrutable, DBT uses practical applications to make it accessible, including tuning into your thoughts, emotions, and physical sensations, mindful breathing, and shifting focus. An essential component of mindfulness practice is observation without judgment, which means greeting the moment as it is without attempting to change it.

DISTRESS TOLERANCE

DBT teaches tangible skills to increase tolerance of distressing situations and emotions, enabling you to move more smoothly through moments of crisis. Distress tolerance can include creating a distraction plan, self-soothing with the five senses, making a pro-con list of the outcomes of acting on urges, and improving the moment with pleasant activities. This might mean distracting yourself by engaging in an activity that requires concentration, by splashing your face with cold water, by listening to soothing music, or by accepting what is out of your control. By preparing for these moments in advance, we can stop reaching for self-destructive behaviors and find healthier ways of coping.

EMOTION REGULATION

The goal of emotion regulation is not to rid yourself of challenging emotions, but to navigate them. Emotions are necessary—they are valuable clues to what is happening in the world around you and in your body. DBT helps you better manage aspects of self-care that can impact our moods, increase your overall awareness of emotions, and act against initial gut reactions to an emotion (a practice called "opposite action"). Anger, for example, might make you want to scream or fight.

Opposite action teaches you to speak quietly and gently. In doing so, you calm your nervous system and subvert old, unhelpful patterns.

INTERPERSONAL EFFECTIVENESS

Studies consistently show that positive relationships protect against stress and negative relationships create stress, worsen immunity, and shorten lifespan.[61][62] Interpersonal effectiveness teaches you to pay attention to your interactions with others in order to maintain or deepen these vital connections. You can develop skills to ask for what you need, set boundaries, actively listen, and negotiate conflict in healthy ways. Learning how to effectively navigate interpersonal situations is an essential part of your psychological well-being.

BUILDING THE LIFE YOU WANT

When we have extreme emotions, act impulsively, or run into conflict with others, it is common to feel racked by shame. We start to believe these emotions, behaviors, and interactions define us. DBT offers a systematic way to examine our patterns and understand why we do what we do, accepting any judgments that arise, so we can make meaningful changes in our lives and relationships.

References

[1] "Depression." *World Health Organization*,
▸ *https://www.who.int/news-room/fact-sheets/detail/depression.*

[2] Watson, Stephanie. "Depression." *Gale Open Access*,
▸ *https://www.gale.com/open-access/depression.*

[3] American Psychiatric Association. *What Is Depression?* Retrieved October 6, 2021, from ▸ *https://www.psychiatry.org/patients-families/depression/what-is-depression.*

[4] *Depression Statistics.* MindWise. (2019, February 18). Retrieved October 6, 2021, from ▸ *https://www.mindwise.org/blog/community/depression-statistics/.*

[5] Burns, D. D. (2009). *Feeling Good.* New York: Harper.

[6] Hagen, E. H. (2011). Evolutionary theories of Depression: A critical review. The Canadian Journal of Psychiatry, 56(12), 716–726.
▸ *https://doi.org/10.1177/070674371105601203*

[7] Sloman, L. (2008). A new comprehensive evolutionary model of depression and anxiety. *Journal of Affective Disorders*, 106(3), 219–228.
▸ *https://doi.org/10.1016/j.jad.2007.07.008*

[8] Kendler, K. S., Karkowski, L. M., & Prescott, C. A. (1998). Stressful life events and major depression: risk period, long-term contextual threat, and diagnostic specificity. *The Journal of nervous and mental disease*, 186(11), 661–669.
▸ *https://doi.org/10.1097/00005053-199811000-00001*

[9] Kendler, K. S., Karkowski, L. M., & Prescott, C. A. (1999). Causal relationship between stressful life events and the onset of major depression. *American Journal of Psychiatry*, 156(6), 837–841.
▸ *https://doi.org/10.1176/ajp.156.6.837*

[10] Dunn, E. C., Brown, R. C., Dai, Y., Rosand, J., Nugent, N. R., Amstadter, A. B., & Smoller, J. W. (2015). Genetic determinants of depression.
Harvard Review of Psychiatry, 23(1), 1–18.
▸ *https://doi.org/10.1097/hrp.0000000000000054*

[11] Krishnan, V., & Nestler, E. J. (2010). Linking molecules to mood: New insight into the biology of depression. *American Journal of Psychiatry*, 167(11), 1305–1320.
▸ *https://doi.org/10.1176/appi.ajp.2009.10030434*

[12] May, R. (2007). *Love and Will.* W.W. Norton.

[13] Freud, S. (1972). *Mourning and Melancholia.*

[14] *Stanford's Sapolsky On Depression in U.S. Youtube.* Retrieved from
▸ *https://www.youtube.com/watch?v=NOAgplgTxfc&t=21s.*

[15] Solomon, A. (2016). *Noonday Demon.* Vintage Publishing.

[16] Insel, T., Cuthbert, B., Garvey, M., Heinssen, R., Pine, D. S., Quinn, K., Sanislow, C., & Wang, P. (2010). Research domain criteria (RDoC): toward a new classification framework for research on mental disorders. *The American Journal of Psychiatry*, 167(7), 748-751. ▸ *doi: 10.1176/appi.ajp.2010.09091379*

[17] Heils, A., Teufel, A., Petri, S., Stöber, G., Riederer, P., Bengel, D., & Lesch, K. P. (2002). Allelic variation of human serotonin transporter gene expression. *Journal of Neurochemistry*, 66(6), 2621–2624.
▸ *https://doi.org/10.1046/j.1471-4159.1996.66062621.x*

[18] Lesch, K.-P., Bengel, D., Heils, A., Sabol, S. Z., Greenberg, B. D., Petri, S., Benjamin, J., Muller, C. R., Hamer, D. H., & Murphy, D. L. (1996). Association of anxiety-related traits with a polymorphism in the serotonin transporter gene regulatory region. *Science*, 274(5292), 1527–1531.
▸ *https://doi.org/10.1126/science.274.5292.1527*

[19] Caspi, A. (2003). Influence of life stress on depression:
Moderation by a polymorphism in the 5-htt gene. *Science*, 301(5631), 386–389.
▸ *https://doi.org/10.1126/science.1083968*

[20] Gariépy, G., Honkaniemi, H., & Quesnel-Vallée, A. (2016). Social support and protection from depression: Systematic review of current findings in Western countries. *British Journal of Psychiatry*, 209(4), 284-293. ▸ *doi:10.1192/bjp. bp.115.169094*

[21] Heiming, R. S., & Sachser, N. (2010). Consequences of serotonin transporter genotype and early adversity on behavioral profile – pathology or adaptation? *Frontiers in Neuroscience*, 4. ▸ *https://doi.org/10.3389/fnins.2010.00187*

[22] Albert, P. (2015). Why is depression more prevalent in women? *Journal of Psychiatry & Neuroscience*, 40(4), 219–221. ▸ *https://doi.org/10.1503/jpn.150205*

[23] Hage, M. P., & Azar, S. T. (2012). The link between thyroid function and Depression. *Journal of Thyroid Research*, 2012, 1–8.
▸ *https://doi.org/10.1155/2012/590648*

[24] Ben Simon, E., Rossi, A., Harvey, A. G., & Walker, M. P. (2019).
Overanxious and underslept. *Nature Human Behaviour*, 4(1), 100–110.
▸ *https://doi.org/10.1038/s41562-019-0754-8*

[25] Lorant, V. (2003). Socioeconomic inequalities in depression:
A meta-analysis. *American Journal of Epidemiology*, 157(2), 98–112.
▸ *https://doi.org/10.1093/aje/kwf182*

[26] Cuijpers, P., Sijbrandij, M., Koole, S. L., Andersson, G., Beekman, A. T., & Reynolds, C. F. (2014). Adding psychotherapy to antidepressant medication in depression and anxiety disorders: A meta-analysis. *World Psychiatry*, 13(1), 56–67.
▸ *https://doi.org/10.1002/wps.20089*

[27] Harris, R. (2009). ACT *Made Simple*. New Harbinger Publications.

[28] Hage, M. P., & Azar, S. T. (2012). The Link between Thyroid Function and Depression. Journal of thyroid research, 2012, 590648.
‣ *https://doi.org/10.1155/2012/590648*

[29] Hölzel, B. K., Carmody, J., Vangel, M., Congleton, C., Yerramsetti, S. M., Gard, T., & Lazar, S. W. (2011). Mindfulness practice leads to increases in regional brain gray matter density. Psychiatry research, 191(1), 36–43.
‣ *https://doi.org/10.1016/j.pscychresns.2010.08.006*

[30] Holt-Lunstad, J., Smith, T. B., & Layton, J. B. (2010). Social relationships and mortality risk: a meta-analytic review. PLoS medicine, 7(7), e1000316.
‣ *https://doi.org/10.1371/journal.pmed.1000316*

[31] Cuijpers, P., Sijbrandij, M., Koole, S. L., Andersson, G., Beekman, A. T., & Reynolds, C. F. (2014). Adding psychotherapy to antidepressant medication in depression and anxiety disorders: A meta-analysis. *World Psychiatry*, 13(1), 56–67.
‣ *https://doi.org/10.1002/wps.20089*

[32] Harris, R., & Hayes, S. (2008). *The Happiness* Trap. Robinson.

[33] A-Tjak, J. G. L., Davis, M. L., Morina, N., Powers, M. B., Smits, J. A. J., & Emmelkamp, P. M. G. (2014). A meta-analysis of the efficacy of acceptance and commitment therapy for clinically relevant mental and physical health problems. *Psychotherapy and Psychosomatics*, 84(1), 30–36.
‣ *https://doi.org/10.1159/000365764*

[34] Gotink, R. A., Meijboom, R., Vernooij, M. W., Smits, M., & Hunink, M. G. M. (2016). 8-week mindfulness based stress reduction induces brain changes similar to traditional long-term meditation practice – a systematic review. *Brain and Cognition*, 108, 32–41. ‣ *https://doi.org/10.1016/j.bandc.2016.07.001*

[35] Tang, Y.-Y., Hölzel, B. K., & Posner, M. I. (2015). The Neuroscience of Mindfulness Meditation. *Nature Reviews Neuroscience*, 16(4), 213–225.
‣ *https://doi.org/10.1038/nrn3916*

[36] Taren, A. A., Creswell, J. D., & Gianaros, P. J. (2013). Dispositional mindfulness co-varies with smaller amygdala and caudate volumes in community adults. *PLoS ONE*, 8(5). ‣ *https://doi.org/10.1371/journal.pone.0064574*

[37] Ford, B. Q., Lam, P., John, O. P., & Mauss, I. B. (2018). The psychological health benefits of accepting negative emotions and thoughts: Laboratory, diary, and longitudinal evidence. *Journal of Personality and Social Psychology,* 115(6), 1075–1092.
‣ *https://doi.org/10.1037/pspp0000157*

[38] Kanter, J. W., Manos, R. C., Bowe, W. M., Baruch, D. E., Busch, A. M., & Rusch, L. C. (2010). What is Behavioral Activation? A Review of the Empirical Literature. *Clinical Psychology Review*, 30(6), 608–620. ‣ *https://doi.org/10.1016/j.cpr.2010.04.001*

[39] Basso, J. C., & Suzuki, W. A. (2017). The effects of acute exercise on mood, cognition, neurophysiology, and neurochemical pathways: A Review. *Brain Plasticity*, 2(2), 127–152. ▸ *https://doi.org/10.3233/bpl-160040*

[40] Jacobson, N. S., Dobson, K. S., Truax, P. A., Addis, M. E., Koerner, K., Gollan, J. K., Gortner, E., & Prince, S. E. (2000). A component analysis of cognitive–behavioral treatment for depression. *Prevention & Treatment*, 3(1). ▸ *https://doi.org/10.1037/1522-3736.3.1.323a*

[41] Dunn, E. C., Brown, R. C., Dai, Y., Rosand, J., Nugent, N. R., Amstadter, A. B., & Smoller, J. W. (2015). Genetic determinants of depression. *Harvard Review of Psychiatry*, 23(1), 1–18. ▸ *https://doi.org/10.1097/hrp.0000000000000054*

[42] Dichter, G. S., Felder, J. N., Petty, C., Bizzell, J., Ernst, M., & Smoski, M. J. (2009). The effects of psychotherapy on neural responses to rewards in major depression. Biological psychiatry, 66(9), 886–897. ▸ *https://doi.org/10.1016/j.biopsych.2009.06.021*

[43] David, D., Cristea, I., & Hofmann, S. G. (2018). Why Cognitive Behavioral Therapy Is the Current Gold Standard of Psychotherapy. Frontiers in psychiatry, 9, 4. ▸ *https://doi.org/10.3389/fpsyt.2018.00004*

[44] Kandel E. R. (2001). The molecular biology of memory storage: a dialogue between genes and synapses. Science (New York, N.Y.), 294(5544), 1030–1038. ▸ *https://doi.org/10.1126/science.1067020*

[45] Eriksson, P. S., Perfilieva, E., Björk-Eriksson, T., Alborn, A. M., Nordborg, C., Peterson, D. A., & Gage, F. H. (1998). Neurogenesis in the adult human hippocampus. Nature medicine, 4(11), 1313–1317. ▸ *https://doi.org/10.1038/3305*

[46] Miu, A. S., & Yeager, D. S. (2014). Preventing symptoms of depression by teaching adolescents that people can change. *Clinical Psychological Science*, 3(5), 726–743. ▸ *https://doi.org/10.1177/2167702614548317*

[47] Yeager, D. S., Hanselman, P., Walton, G. M., Murray, J. S., Crosnoe, R., Muller, C., Tipton, E., Schneider, B., Hulleman, C. S., Hinojosa, C. P., Paunesku, D., Romero, C., Flint, K., Roberts, A., Trott, J., Iachan, R., Buontempo, J., Yang, S. M., Carvalho, C. M., ... Dweck, C. S. (2019). A national experiment reveals where a growth mindset improves achievement. *Nature*, 573(7774), 364–369. ▸ *https://doi.org/10.1038/s41586-019-1466-y*

[48] Schleider, J., & Weisz, J. (2017). A single-session growth mindset intervention for adolescent anxiety and depression: 9-month outcomes of a randomized trial. *Journal of Child Psychology and Psychiatry*, 59(2), 160–170. ▸ *https://doi.org/10.1111/jcpp.12811*

[49] Seligman M. E. (1978). Learned helplessness as a model of depression. Comment and integration. Journal of abnormal psychology, 87(1), 165–179.

[50] Dweck, C. S., & Yeager, D. S. (2019). Mindsets: A View From Two Eras. Perspectives on psychological science : a journal of the Association for Psychological Science, 14(3), 481–496. ‣ https://doi.org/10.1177/1745691618804166

[51] Werner, A. M., Tibubos, A. N., Rohrmann, S., & Reiss, N. (2019). The clinical trait self-criticism and its relation to psychopathology: A systematic review - Update. Journal of affective disorders, 246, 530–547. ‣ https://doi.org/10.1016/j.jad.2018.12.069

[52] Germer, C. K., & Neff, K. D. (2013). Self-compassion in clinical practice. Journal of clinical psychology, 69(8), 856–867. ‣ https://doi.org/10.1002/jclp.22021

[53] López, A., Sanderman, R., & Schroevers, M. J. (2018). A close examination of the relationship between self-compassion and depressive symptoms. Mindfulness, 9(5), 1470–1478. ‣ https://doi.org/10.1007/s12671-018-0891-6

[54] Körner, A., Coroiu, A., Copeland, L., Gomez-Garibello, C., Albani, C., Zenger, M., & Brähler, E. (2015). The Role of Self-Compassion in Buffering Symptoms of Depression in the General Population. PloS one, 10(10), e0136598. ‣ https://doi.org/10.1371/journal.pone.0136598

[55] Ost L. G. (2008). Efficacy of the third wave of behavioral therapies: a systematic review and meta-analysis. Behaviour research and therapy, 46(3), 296–321. ‣ https://doi.org/10.1016/j.brat.2007.12.005

[56] Thomas R. Lynch; Alexander L. Chapman; M. Zachary Rosenthal; Janice R. Kuo; Marsha M. Linehan (2006). Mechanisms of change in dialectical behavior therapy: Theoretical and empirical observations. , 62(4), 459–480. ‣ doi:10.1002/jclp.20243

[57] Panos, P. T., Jackson, J. W., Hasan, O., & Panos, A. (2014). Meta-Analysis and Systematic Review Assessing the Efficacy of Dialectical Behavior Therapy (DBT). Research on social work practice, 24(2), 213–223. ‣ https://doi.org/10.1177/1049731513503047

[58] Bankoff, S. M., Karpel, M. G., Forbes, H. E., & Pantalone, D. W. (2012). A systematic review of dialectical behavior therapy for the treatment of eating disorders. Eating disorders, 20(3), 196–215. ‣ https://doi.org/10.1080/10640266.2012.668478

[59] Valentine, S. E., Bankoff, S. M., Poulin, R. M., Reidler, E. B., & Pantalone, D. W. (2015). The use of dialectical behavior therapy skills training as stand-alone treatment: a systematic review of the treatment outcome literature. Journal of clinical psychology, 71(1), 1–20. ‣ https://doi.org/10.1002/jclp.22114

[60] Dimeff, L., & Linehan, M.M. (2001). Dialectical behavior therapy in a nutshell. The California Psychologist, 34, 10-13

[61] Yang, Y. C., Boen, C., Gerken, K., Li, T., Schorpp, K., & Harris, K. M. (2016). Social relationships and physiological determinants of longevity across the human life span. *Proceedings of the National Academy of Sciences*, 113(3), 578–583. ▸ *https://doi.org/10.1073/pnas.1511085112*

[62] Holt-Lunstad, J., Smith, T. B., & Layton, J. B. (2010). Social relationships and mortality risk: a meta-analytic review. PLoS medicine, 7(7), e1000316. ▸ *https://doi.org/10.1371/journal.pmed.1000316*